W9-BZX-766

TRIAL & ERROR

TRIAL & ERROR

The Education
of a
Freedom Lawyer

prose poems by
Arthur W. Campbell

Volume One:

For the Defense

Poetic Matrix Press

© 2007 by Arthur W. Campbell

Written copyright licenses liberally granted.
Contact author c/o
California Western School of Law
225 Cedar Street
San Diego, CA 92101
Phone: 619-525-1450
Edress: acampbell@cwsl.edu

ISBN 978-09789597-4-6

All rights reserved. No part of this book may be used or
reproduced in any manner without written permission,
except in the case of quotes for personal use and brief
quotations embodied in critical articles or reviews.

Poetic Matrix Press
P.O. Box 1223
Madera, CA 93639
www.poeticmatrix.com
poeticmatrix@yahoo.com

"The truth is rarely pure and never simple."
— George Bernard Shaw

"There is so little to say
and so much time to say it in."
— Charles Wright

CONTENT

This volume is dedicated
to Thomas Lester Cummings
and Drusilla Newlon Campbell:
two great teachers in my life.

PREFACE

What are freedom lawyers? They come in all sizes, ages, genders, and eras. They come with an array of different talents and interests. They labor in all areas of society. What they all possess is steadfast determination to oppose injustice wherever it appears.

Since I chose the criminal courtroom as my battlefield, I had the chance to fight for the freedoms of all Americans: the freedom from unwarranted arrests, unreasonable searches, coerced confessions, vindictive prosecutions, unfair trials, and irrational sentences. In short, for each citizen's right to justice.

Discovering precisely where injustice lay in each client's case took me far beyond what I could learn from legal treatises. Learning to fight it effectively took many frustrating lessons of trial and error in many forums on behalf of many clients.

Though each case taught me more about effective advocacy, my clients paid for these lessons by placing their freedom in my hands. These are their stories as much as mine.

FOREWORD

By Charles M. Sevilla, Esq.

Author of WILKES: HIS LIFE AND CRIMES; WILKES ON TRIAL; and DISORDER IN THE COURT: GREAT FRACTURED MOMENTS IN COURTROOM HISTORY.

Professor Campbell has scored a literary hat trick. He's written a work that appeals to the general public, attorneys, and readers of poetry. An experienced trial lawyer and accomplished poet, in *TRIAL & ERROR* Campbell candidly reveals the courtroom life: its ordeals, surprises, defeats, and triumphs. This volume—the first of a planned trilogy—is about the practical education of a young freedom lawyer.

Prior to graduating from law school, Campbell represented clients before a rural justice of the peace, a small-town judge, and a state administrative agency. He takes the reader into those offbeat arenas, culminating in his experience as the country's first law student to argue before a state supreme court.

He next takes the reader through his first year as a practicing lawyer, where he defended indigent clients in one of the nation's roughest criminal-law jurisdictions, the District of Columbia. I know. I was there at the time.

Campbell opens to the public a level of lawyering seldom revealed in conventional media: the painstaking process by which attorneys build cases for clients, sometimes against hopeless odds, witness by witness, motion by motion, point by point, always alert for unplanned developments that can win or sink the case.

Young or aspiring lawyers can read of Campbell's experiences and find not only useful strategies and tactics but also reassurance that hard work and dedication can steer one through daunting times. Seasoned litigators will enjoy Campbell's ingenuity during unexpected courtroom moments, his wry observations, and steady improvement through post-trial reflections.

For poetry readers Campbell captures a wide range of emotion, perspective, and resonance. Each prose poem stretches vivid images across a different thematic loom, weaving disparate threads into a finished story. This is a highly enjoyable ride.

INTRODUCTION

Clutching a degree from Harvard and dreams of Clarence Darrow, I enrolled in law school. I was lucky to attend during the launch of a student-practice rule that allowed me to represent real clients my third year.

After graduation from law school I received an E. Barrett Prettyman fellowship from Georgetown University's Law Center. There I worked my way through a Masters of Criminal Justice in a program that exposed me to practice in reverse of the usual career sequence: first as defense counsel, then as a Special Assistant United States Attorney.

This volume covers my first experiences as a freedom lawyer. Spanning my months from law-student litigator to fledgling attorney, it's derived from personal notes preserved apart from client files. Many insights from these cases—the *why's* beneath the *what's*—weren't realized until long after gavels struck wood. When I actually stood in court facing dismal options, sometimes all I could do was fall back on the advice of attorney-poet Wallace Stevens; I tried to fashion silk scarves from the viscera of worms.

George Bernard Shaw often quipped, "Those who can, do. Those who can't, teach." As one who now teaches law, I've got a Shavian rebuttal: "Those who do and *then* teach, gain perspective."

My journey as a freedom lawyer started with naive beliefs that "right makes might," that courts sought only truth, and all judges strove for justice. As I fought for my clients' various rights, I gradually abandoned my King Arthur fantasies for more realistic views. I augmented swords and lances with modern advocacy tools.

Clients walk through these pages in the order by which they walked into my office or were assigned to me by court. Most of their names have been changed to protect, if not their innocence, their privacy. Their actual names sometimes appear where cases climbed from courthouse dockets to the news. Even with these, however, I've taken care to reveal no client's secrets or confidences. On the other hand, the names of many associates and investigators are real—small recognition for their considerable help and guidance.

Against my wish for historical accuracy, colleagues persuaded me to fictionalize names of the most bungling, self-righteous, and blindly ambitious police, prosecutors, and judges. Although I'd stand firmly on truth against any charge of defamation, by now witnesses to their staggering incompetence would be difficult to assemble.

Two points on terminology. First, these poems portray the "courthouse process," a more realistic label than our culture's ironic euphemism, "criminal justice." The gulf between these two concepts is especially poignant in "The Thanksgiving Addict," my first felony case in Washington, D.C.

Second, I don't refer to prosecutors as "the government" or "the people." Regarding the former term, seldom did I encounter prosecutorial positions that reflected all three branches of our republic. As for the latter, I considered most of my clients closer to "the people" than those who wanted to lock them up.

As a budding litigator I was neither eloquent nor at ease with public speaking. What I brought to court, however, seemed often in short supply: facts, perseverance, and passion. I strongly believed in the adversary system and—despite my lack of skill and experience—made sure at least I was prepared.

While on sabbatical in the 1990s, I wrote to scores of published poet-lawyers. Where could I find their poems on justice or travails in court? Did they have unpublished work to share? My correspondents included law professors, ambassadors, ministers of justice, legislators, and two nations' presidents. Only Martin Espada, a freedom lawyer in the field of poverty law, admitted that he'd even *written* poems about law.

Surprised and dismayed, I wondered if their days as lawyers were so bereft of insights into human freedom, so devoid of struggle and emotion, that they held no poetic potential. One day, I promised myself, I'd share some of the dramas that danced through my years in court.

The Education
of a
Freedom Lawyer

ROCKY MOUNTAIN EQUITY

Generally speaking, you aren't learning much
when your lips are moving. — Contemporary Zen

Male mutters ricocheted through Squire Bobble's foyer.
Fourteen angry mountaineers bumped elbows, scooted
chairs, and stroked their stubbled chins. Finally they
collected in two rustling clumps, half around complainant
Gus Swart, the rest beside Clive Ritter and his counsel: me.

Charged with breaching the peace, Clive was summoned
to a forum as ancient as its name was apt: county justice
of the peace. He was my first client, I a senior in my law
school clinic's maiden year.

Aged 32, Clive packed 180 pounds around a five-eleven
frame. He'd tucked an ironed yellow shirt inside his best
black slacks.

Gus outweighed Clive by forty pounds. He drew his
leather face into a scowl above a blue-checked shirt and
faded jeans. The toes of his brown work boots had been
scuffed to mustard hues.

Suddenly the office door swung open. "Who are you?"
Squire Bobble growled, squinting from 300 pounds of flesh
stuffed in a turquoise, threadbare dress. Her eyes had
locked on me. I gulped, clambered to my feet,
announced, "Law student representing the defendant."

"This ain't no federal case," she scoffed, "but you all
come in, let's get on." Bobble turned, marched to her
pinewood desk, and eased onto a creaking chair.

3

The crowd shuffled through the inner doorway of her office-court, rented space above a dry goods store. Before her desk were only chairs for two; in the corner stood a hip-high wooden stool.

"What witnesses need sworn?" inquired the squire. Fourteen burly arms grabbed air. She arched an eyebrow, pledged them to the truth *en masse.*

"What's complainant got to say?"

Gus Swart took three steps forward, planted his right foot, then shifted most his weight to it. "Yer honor, I was walking home from the mill last month when Ritter come up along side and punched me in the jaw."

"That's a lie!" retorted Clive.

"No it ain't!" yelled three of Gus' folks.

"'Tis so!" roared all Clive's people, edging to the wall on Squire's right. Complainant's friends seized space along her left.

I raised my eyebrows at the squire, hoping she would quell this budding melee. She grimaced, nodded to me: "It's your case, counselor. Let's proceed."

I grabbed the wooden stool, banged it down between the shouting groups. Raising both my arms palms out, I bellowed, "Okay, guys, hold on a sec!"

Like a high-school band conductor I propped my butt against the stool, faced complainant's crowd, and smiled, "Why don't you go first?"

They did, altogether for three minutes, til the squire stared at her worn green carpet, shook her head, raised one massive arm.

I turned to the squire: "Now my side's turn, your honor?"

She sighed, nodded, closed her eyes. I swiveled on the stool until I faced my client's witnesses. They burst forth at once, ignoring my pretrial prep. Their babble escalated as one emphasized his clearer view, another Ritter's innocence, complainant's year-old grudge.

All I could do was hope our louder clamor would persuade the squire. I knew she'd need widespread support come next fall's elections. Her way of maximizing votes, however, was so shrewd its lawlessness at first shot past my head.

Bobble stood; the din collapsed. In a tone that froze all opposition, she declared, "I find defendant Ritter not guilty and assess him all court fees and costs."

I thought, *all right—your career's first victory!* Then my mind caught up and whispered, *Whoa! How did her verdict end?* I stood up from my stool and faced the squire.

"Your honor," I objected, "fees and costs are more than Mr. Ritter's fine would be if he were guilty of this crime." Fishing in my briefcase, I tugged out a copy of the state constitution, showed her where it clearly outlawed split decisions of this sort.

Bobble seized the document, glared at it for seven seconds. Then she pursed her lips and drawled, "Counselor, looks like I'll have to reconsider my verdict." She clapped both palms upon her hips, raised three jiggling chins, held my gaze with hers.

Outrage leapt like wolves inside my throat. I took a long breath, scoured my mind for some point of law to pierce her armor of authority. Ritter tugged my arm, desperation scrawled across his face:"Mr. Campbell, that's all right, I'll pay!"

Swart's supporters nodded fiercely, stamped down the stairs, grumbled up the street.

Clive's crew filed from the courtroom, leaving him and me with Bobble. My client spread his dollars on the squire's desk, crumpled her receipt inside the pocket of his slacks.

When Clive and I walked down the steps and blinked into the light, our witnesses engulfed us. They slapped our backs and whooped,"We won, we won! Sure showed that son of a bitch!"

I smiled gamely, not sure what we'd showed or won. What surged through my mind was that I had a lot to learn about the way law really worked, more than I'd absorbed from books, films, court opinions, and lectures on the law.

In hindsight I see Squire Bobble as my first teacher in the school of freedom law. She previewed what I'd need to understand to be a more effective advocate.

Much time would pass before I put aside my views that courtroom combat always pitted good guys against bad, lined up wholly right against dead wrong, and let just one side win.

It took weeks for me to recognize law's halls often opened onto paradox, that I must master subtlety to move my clients' cases through its twisting corridors.

It took me longer to accept that law was constantly arm-wrestling with power, that without some muscle in the grip of freedom's advocate, naked power won.

Looking back, I see the outcome of my first trial from different points of view. From a "realpolitik" perspective the verdict in Clive's favor showed which side of a small-town squabble could muster more intensity. From a "vindication" standpoint, both Clive's and Alan's folks danced the victor's tune.

But that day's trophy for "win-win" went to the participant with power. The squire stuffed more cash inside her safe and next spring commandeered two extra blocks of votes. With flair and intuition Squire Bobble packed all these points of view into one bag of Rocky Mountain equity.

SURPRISED IN CHAMBERS

Some judges are like the old bishop
who, having begun to eat asparagus at
the wrong end, did not choose to alter.
— Lord Pitfour (1768)

"Judge Fetlock, please release Shane Melkoff. He's been cooped in jail for three whole months. He's trapped because he couldn't post the peace bond that his wife took out on him."

Shane slumped beside me in a chair, black hair cascading over hazel eyes above a jutting jaw. His handcuffs had been doffed by a lanky sheriff's deputy who now stood one lunge-length behind his chair.

I bent and whispered, "Shane, sit up!" As my thirty-year-old client straightened, he revealed a wet blotch of coffee on the placket of his once-white shirt.

Professor Bradford Tomlinson stood beside us as my supervising attorney, a requirement for student-lawyering before all courts of record in the state. He wore a tailored, dark-blue, three-piece suit. I'd donned the only suit I owned: black, two-piece, off-the-rack, pressed so much it shined.

"Your honor, Mr. Melkoff wants to reconcile with his wife, his employer says he'll take him back, plus he needs surgery for his knee."

My words drew strength from my conviction in their cause. As I'd researched the local peace-bond law, elemental questions shadowed me: *What's the sense of spending county funds to lock up citizens too poor to pay a bond to back their pledge of peace? Why next charge them room and board? Won't that further pauperize their family, throw more thumbtacks on the bedroom floor?*

If Shane's confiscated billfold merely clutched a valid credit card—that is, if he'd been middle class—he could have turned the key inside his 8-by-10-foot cell and walked out free.

But today I wouldn't argue peace bonds were so senseless and unfair they were unconstitutional. My client didn't want to be the poster boy for a protracted siege against the system. Shane just wanted out.

So I anchored Shane's case in plain pragmatic ground: "Judge, it's impossible for Mr. Melkoff to post a bond. The court's own file proves his poverty; there's his affidavit. Plus, the state's new student-practice rule only lets me act for clients who are indigent."

I added one ironic fact I hoped would tweak a nerve of justice in the judge. "Last week his mother tried to post his bond but Sheriff Kram refused to let him out til someone pays three-hundred dollars more for Mr. Melkoff's extended stay in jail."

I sat down, asked myself, *Wasn't that convincing? How could the D.A. refute these facts?*

The district attorney gripped the silver handle of his sable cane, slowly pushed out of his chair. At fifty, Lonnie Patella wore his auburn hair swept back, striving for a look of wisdom on his brawny six-foot-two-inch frame. His grey three-piece suit shed every wrinkle when he stood.

"The State would like to call one witness for the court." Patella aimed his forefinger at Maurice Bowdin—the only witness I had brought to testify for Shane!

I'd subpoenaed Bowdin, Shane's confidant and next-door neighbor, to tell the judge how much my client loved his high-school sweetheart bride; that Shane had shared specifics of a reconciliation plan with him. (Details would be hearsay but the plan would show my client's state of mind.)

Maurice clambered to the stand, left cheek baggy from three decades churning wads of Mail Pouch tobacco. Patella asked him to admit that Shane was known throughout the town for starting fights from paltry provocations.

I leapt to my feet: "Objection! That's irrelevant to what goes on inside my client's home...."

"Overruled," droned Fetlock without glancing my direction. I sat down, bit my lip, wondered if a seasoned lawyer would foresee an ambush of this sort.

Judge Dewey Fetlock's deeply crevassed face hinged his age at fifty-five, allowed a ten-year swing on either side. I thought, *It's clear he doesn't welcome student lawyers in his court, but why does he appear so bored?"*

At the judge's nod to him, Maurice responded to Patella's query. "Well, I've heard people say Shane sometimes gets a little feisty."

His point made, Patella sat down, shuffled through a file on his table. But as I rose to start my questions for Maurice, Patella launched two more torpedoes.

"Does Your honor know that Mr. Melkoff has outstanding warrants—one for writing a bad check, another for possessing copper wire without a receipt?"

(The copper-wire statute was the spawn of Mama Bell and Redi Kilowatt. They used it to protect gigantic rolls of wire stacked beside their towers as they stretched electron highways over Rocky Mountain spines.)

Seizing law-school logic, I tried muffling the explosion from Patella's prejudicial and improper claims. "First, as your honor knows, Mr. Melkoff is presumed innocent of these accusations. Second, there's no domestic violence behind either charge."

10

The judge looked at Patella for response; the prosecutor met his gaze but otherwise sat mute on his polished chair. Fetlock unpropped his chin from a sling of boney knuckles. In a singsong voice he said he'd heard enough: "Motion to release: denied."

Maurice Bowdin stepped down from the witness chair, passed me with his raised eyebrows as if to say, "Why won't he let me testify to all those good things about Shane?"

In response I shook my head, stared at the pile of unused documents on my table: witness questions, affidavits, statutes, case citations, notes for further arguments. If only I had checked all courthouse records of my client!

My mind flashed on the case I'd tried in front of Squire Bobble. Do judges also use raw power to blithely brush the law aside?

Then Fetlock cleared his throat and boomed through post-adjudication silence. His proclamation made me realize no facts, law, or logic could have loosed his grasp on one side of this case. "This town is better off with Melkoff in its jail!"

DELAYED ASSISTANCE

*Good judgment comes from bad experience,
and a lot of that comes from bad judgment.*
— Will Rogers

The law gave Welfare forty-five days to signal green or red
on citizen requests for aid. Darrell Worster had been
waiting for five months when he limped through the
doorway of our law school clinic.

As I shook his outstretched hand, he smiled meekly: a pallid
man of fifty-three, worn beyond his years. We discussed his
situation as I jotted notes. Darrell signed the necessary
forms to let me take his case, said good-bye, and eased his
body out the door.

For an hour I researched the law, then walked to the
Welfare Office, thumbed through Darrell's file. It
wallowed in bureaucratese. The title page had suffered
torture in the Hall of Obfuscation: "Application for Aid
to the Disabled Assistance."

I waded through its technicode, took notes, walked back
to Legal Aid, and prepared Darrell Worster's case.

Shields clanged with lances in my mind as I outlined our
points of law, matched them to the entries I had found in
Welfare's file, armed myself to battle the bureaucracy. In
light of Welfare's dragging feet, our petition rang with irony:
"A Hearing to Accelerate Relief."

On hearing day my client, another supervising lawyer, and I
gathered in the waiting room of Gene L. Brisket, Welfare
Hearing Officer. We perched on folding metal chairs whose
tube legs splayed above a floor of cracked linoleum tile.

"Come in," Brisket warbled, swinging wide his office door. We shook hands, introduced ourselves, debated briefly how much snow would fall that night. When Brisket stepped behind his desk and sat, we eased onto three wooden chairs in front of him.

My supervisor nodded at me to proceed. With a practiced Perry Mason smile, I challenged the customary way such hearings ran. As hearing officer, how could Brisket sit in judgment of my client's case and at the same time act as advocate for Welfare's side?

From Brisket's stunned expression I surmised no one had ever raised this point of elemental fairness, at least no needy supplicant before his throne of power.

Blood shot through Brisket's temples as he searched for a response. For half a minute he leafed through Welfare's file on Darrell. When he raised his head, his solemn tone could not disguise the fact he'd only found the obvious.

"Well, Mr. Campbell, the report does seem...to indicate...delay in processing your client's application..."

Suddenly he beamed as if he'd stumbled onto file-folder gold: "...consequently no officer was requested to present Welfare's position."

It took a moment to digest Brisket's triumphant non sequitur. Then I peered beneath his smoke: *Has he just admitted his department caused the holdup in this case? Have we already won the major fight? Should I put away my documents, argue only how much back-pay Darrell is owed?*

Oops, better try to nail down this statement, lest Brisket later try to brush it off like Squire Bobble threatened in Clive Ritter's case.

"Can we turn on the tape recorder?" I asked, nodding to the instrument asleep on Brisket's desk.

"Hearings *can* be taped...," he said through thin-stretched lips, glanced at the book of regulations crouching near his table lamp. Mock-smiling, he concluded, "...but it's not required. Mr. Campbell, do you care to proceed?"

Suppressing my frustration, I decided to present the case as if we still must prove all the delays were Welfare's fault. I laid out crucial dates, each backstopped by a paper nesting inside Brisket's file:

♦ Day 1: Darrell applies for help.

♦ Day 45: Deadline passes with no Agency response.

♦ Day 58: Darrell falls unconscious at work, rushed by ambulance to hospital.

♦ Day 62: Agency doctor refuses to examine Darrell; schedules exam by another doctor for Day 83.

♦ Day 83: No entry made in Welfare files.

♦ Day 100: X-rays taken, billed to Darrell.

♦ Day 105: Agency worker dictates Darrell's case summary.

♦ Day 175: (just after I'd requested to examine Darrell's file) Agency Review Team states it "needs more facts."

The moment I closed Welfare's self-confessing calendar, Brisket pounced: "So, your client *worked* for two months after he applied for aid?"

"Yes, of course. His family had to eat while they were waiting word from you." Brisket frowned. "Too bad. I'm resetting Worster's application time to the date when he was hospitalized."

Brisket leaned back in his chair, then cast the *coup de grace*: "I'll recommend back pay forty-five days from then. Let's see...that would place it at day one-hundred-three... but only if our Agency Review Team approves. Now, Mr. Campbell, would you like to file an appeal?"

I felt my stomach tighten but held back my mounting anger.
"We'll have to determine that, sir, after your Review Team acts."
I raised my brows for guidance from my supervisor. He
dropped his gaze, shook his head, indicating nothing
more to do or say.

As we exited the hearing room, Darrell matched his
syncopated stride to mine, motioned me to bend my head
toward his, then whispered timidly, "Thank you,
Mr. Campbell. You did all you could."

Driving home that afternoon on winding mountain roads,
I squinted through my snow-blurred windshield. A cloud
shaped like Justice and her scales hung near the horizon.
I asked her, "Am I crazy, fighting city hall?"

"Hell no!" she retorted. "It *must* be fought, our public
servants held accountable!" Then she winked, "But don't
forget that you won't always win."

Weeks later I mulled over what I'd won for Darrell Worster:
welfare payments after 103 days instead of 45. Did I take
that adversarial stance with Brisket because my dreams of
lawyering required good knights always fight with bad?

Or had watching law get slammed by power in my first two
cases tweak my wariness, heighten my distrust for figures
of authority? Did clapping on a knighthood visor blind me
to the greater gains I might have won for Darrell?

What if I had laid my sword beside my chair, donned a
problem-solving attitude? When I challenged Brisket on his
fairness and recording did I make the classic slip of
youthful warriors—make a battle out of everything, and
then fight too hard?

WOODSTOCK'S TRILOGY

PART ONE: INITIAL APPEARANCE

*There are two kinds of lawyers: Those who know the
law and those who know the judge.* — Anonymous

"*Address?* Woodstock, U.S.A.," says my seventeen-year-old
client when I greet him in the jail's conference room.
Penniless, disowned by parents at age four, he's accused
of stealing twelve bucks worth of food from St. Clarissa's
coffeehouse.

Pastor Rowley told the District Attorney that St. Clarissa's
preferred not to press charges. But they got pressed—
and hard. It took time to find out why.

Last term of court Woodstock roused a growl from Judge
Dewey Fetlock. In an interview the grizzled jurist
grumbled he was forced to dismiss Woodstock's prior
pot-possession charge upon a "technicality."

To law-and-order demagogues that word means "law that
I don't like," usually the Bill of Rights.

For three weeks this term Woodstock has been locked up
with adults in county jail, unable to post bail, secure a trial
date, or get the D.A. to dismiss his charge of petty theft.

Assisted by my supervisor, I draft and file three pleadings
on Woodstock's behalf: (1) Let him, a pauper, proceed
without court costs or fees; (2) Let me represent him;
(3) Grant him bail on personal recognizance until his trial.

Despite contrary inclinations, Judge Fetlock can't refuse the
first request. The U.S. Supreme Court made it clear that
indigents get equal access to our courts.

16

My second pleading makes the judge leaf through the
courthouse file before him, scrutinize my client's affidavits.
He knows the student-practice rule is "new," "untested."
Scary tags for arch conservatives.

"Are you sure you want a *student* as your lawyer?" Fetlock
asks. "Okay by me," chimes Woodstock with a shrug.

"The state has no problem with Mr. Campbell's first two
requests," drawls prosecutor Lonnie Patella, leaning on the
cane he's flourished since the day his shed blew up with
him inside.

Thinking my last plea, bail on a petty charge, would be an
easy victory, I'm surprised it changes to a gauntlet on the
courtroom floor. Patella continues, "... but the state objects
to personal recognizance. We'll need a monetary bail."

Fetlock stares intently at his file. In my mind I see him
blanch at next day's morning news:

    JUDGE TURNS WOODSTOCK LOOSE AGAIN:
    FREE SPIRIT SPRUNG BY STUDENT LAWYER.

I recall a rumor I'd laughed at when it surfaced in my
search for background facts: *Patella wants to ratchet
Woodstock's time in jail, wring out what the kid's supposed
to know about a jealous husband's blowing up the D.A.'s
shed while Patella was inside.*

Great Scot! I wonder now. *Did this rumor snag some truth?*

I rise to my feet, roll out law and logic. First: state and
federal constitutions require "reasonable" bail. Second: I
invite Judge Fetlock to reflect upon his prior rulings. If
Woodstock can't pay court fees or a lawyer, how could
any money bail be reasonable?

17

Next I point to facts that show my client doesn't pose a risk of flight. Except for two years of his life, Woodstock's lived in this small town with sundry family members or foster parents. St. Clarissa's Parish has promised him a place to sleep; a social worker volunteered to act as his official contact with the court.

Gaining confidence from what feels like a perfect wave of arguments, I draw the court's attention to a phrase reclining on page two of my written motion: "Woodstock has no prior juvenile or criminal record."

In the world of legal theory this assertion's true: courts should only recognize a crime that's proved inside their halls, not allegations made by cops and prosecutors, those who hang their suits outside on stubs of the executive branch.

But the judge's world has little truck with legal theory. The thin-faced jurist stares for fifteen seconds at this page, draws his lips into a horizontal line. His vision narrows til it seems to view my client as Patella does: grocery bandit, threat to local teenage morals, suppressor of explosive evidence.

Fetlock clears his throat, opines, "I've got discretion here?" He looks for reassurance at Patella. The latter settles in his chair, says nothing, simply nods.

"All right, the Court sets bail at one-thousand dollars."

I jump to my feet. "But, your honor, for a pauper that's impossible! It amounts to no bail at all!"

"That's my ruling," he declares, slaps shut the courthouse file: "Case closed." Fetlock hoists his cotton robe an inch above brown crepe-soled shoes, strides quickly from the court.

Patella smirks at me with a paternal tilt of brows: "Would you like practice drafting the judge's bail order?"

"You won it, you write it," I retort with heat. His grin broadens, then with dripping condescension he appends,"The state feels it doesn't win *or* lose in matters such as these."

PART TWO: JUVENILE JURISDICTION

Judges are the weakest link in our system of
justice. They are also the most protected.
— Alan Dershowitz

Last week Judge Fetlock refused to free my 17 year-old client on bail. Woodstock's languished for a month in county lockup with adults. Today I'll return to Fetlock's court, armed with witnesses and motions.

It's time to press a novel argument concerning Woodstock's age and the charge he stole twelve-dollars worth of food: If preliminary evidence shows this juvenile should be tried as an adult, such evidence should be found by jurors, not a judge.

State code lets a jury ascertain all facts in juvenile trials. Thus, the threshold question—what type of trial to convene—should likewise rest on juried facts.

Woodstock wants a juvenile trial. When D.A.s win such cases, kids are only found "delinquent," ordered to "reform," all records later sealed. In adult court they're found "guilty," then get "sentenced," lug a rap-sheet all their life.

This will be our legal clinic's shot to make new law. What's more, a hearing on our motion will disclose the weakness of the D.A.'s case, reinforce my prior argument that Woodstock should at least be out on bail.

At home I don my tired suit, drive to the law school, gulp two cups of tepid coffee in the student lounge. With me is Hal Cuffdon, a professor who once took on F. Lee Bailey in a military court.

19

Professor Cuffdon, in his stylish dark-brown suit, volunteered as supervisor for today. "Don't get rattled, Art, if Fetlock doesn't buy your arguments. Just state the first one, make your record, move on to the next."

My mind darts to the legal ethics class I'll miss so I can spend today in court. The textbook slumbers in my briefcase; I can study if we get delayed. But that tome hasn't touched upon the ways law bends to power in this mountain town.

When I began defending poor folks as a freedom lawyer, I fancied I'd be David, going toe-to-toe with various Goliaths. But that fantasy collapsed when power-brokers changed the rules mid-battle, brushed aside my righteous missiles, gave me cheap shots in return.

Cuffdon and I walk to the courthouse, check in with the judge's clerk, wait inside the courtroom til the bailiff sounds the low-high chant, "All rise!"

Dewey Fetlock enters from his private door behind the bench, dispenses nods to the D.A., Professor Cuffdon, half of one to me.

"Be seated," he declares. As we do, the clerk announces Woodstock's case.

I stand and summarize our motion. Judge Fetlock's eyes begin to glaze but I take solace from the fact I'm only laying groundwork for appeal.

I conclude and ask if I can answer any questions for the court. Fetlock shakes his head, starts thumbing through my motion's lengthy memorandum of authorities. As I sit down, coffee rumbles in my gut.

Instead of having the D.A. respond to my arguments,
Fetlock frowns, stares out a window on the right side of his
bench. As if lost in thought for several moments he
declares, "The court denies defendant's motion."

I look at Professor Cuffdon; his eyebrows raise minutely,
shoulders yield the slightest shrug. What I don't expect
develops next.

On the likelihood we'd lose this motion, we calendared
the rest of court this morning for the judge to hear our
evidence that Woodstock's trial should take place in
juvenile court.

As procedure for this hearing, I announce our first position:
"The burden falls on the D.A. to prove our client is
unusually mature, or the alleged theft of groceries is so
dangerous a crime that he must stand trial as an adult."

Lest our hearing bog down on procedure, I add,
"Nonetheless, we've brought the court five witnesses to
show he should be treated as a juvenile."

Fellow students in the clinic had tracked down,
interviewed, and persuaded these fine folks to miss a day
of work and testify for Woodstock, even drove them to
the courthouse steps. They'll vouch for Woodstock's
gentleness, naivete, how he always tries to please,
sometimes stumbles over tough decisions.

District Attorney Patella rises, pivots on his cane, peers
around the courtroom, surveys my squad of witnesses.
From the front row smiles a woman in a dress of forest
green. Beside her sits a man in pressed tan shirt and slacks,
his shock of red hair barely tamed by Brylcreem. Three
other neatly dressed adults appear behind these two.

Patella strikes a look of tragic disappointment: "Your honor," he asserts, "the State requests a week's continuance. Its single witness is not present."

Indignation wrestles fear inside my mind: *If Fetlock doesn't hear our evidence today I'll never get our witnesses to dress for court again and lose another day of work.*

My voice rises half an octave. "The D.A.'s single witness flouts the court's subpoena! I respectfully request your honor issue a bench warrant for this person. Defense will yield an hour's delay for a deputy to bring this shirking witness into court."

I suspect Patella's bluffing but I'm fairly sure he won't admit he failed to subpoena a would-be crucial witness for his case.

However, Patella offers no response to my request and offer, no excuse, no naming of the witness, no proffer of expected testimony. He just sits down, folds his hands, and stares intently at the judge.

Fetlock gets the message. "Since the State must bear the burden to prove juvenile-court waiver, I grant the State's request."

Woodstock flashes me his customary grin as he's handcuffed for return to life in jail. Our five witnesses stand up, shake their heads, start straggling out of court. I catch up, thank them for their patience, hope they'll come another day. They toss me hollow smiles.

Angry and dismayed, I trudge back to law school with Professor Cuffdon. A winter sky coats the horizon with a film of gloomy gray. Wind kicks shriveled maple leaves against our trouser cuffs.

I ask if there was something more I should have done or said. "Don't feel bad," the law prof says. "You did okay. Oh, remember, never slide your papers across the bench to a judge. Hand them to the bailiff or the courtroom clerk."

I grit my teeth for muffing basic courtroom etiquette, stare at sidewalk cracks as we proceed in silence. Surely there is more ex-trial-lawyer Cuffdon can explain about events in court today.

Perhaps he feels my need for more perspective, to know that something positive emerged from all our efforts. What he says, however, merely strengthens lessons I've been learning as a student litigator. "Well, Art, you've just seen how small-town politics runs on the abuse of public trust by public servants with discretionary power."

"Absolutely," I reply. From only five weeks practice in this town, my list of public trolls includes a justice of the peace, the sheriff, sundry bureaucrats, the D.A., and one judge.

I turn to Cuffdon. "Guess our clinic isn't winning any points from the establishment, challenging the status quo for folks with legal rights but not a pocketful of clout."

"That's true," he says. "The good old boys won't give us any points and our impoverished clients haven't any points to give. But the clinic's showing you and fellow students how law works or fails to work in real people's lives."

"Plus," he pauses til I catch the twinkle in his eye, "every now and then we do a little good."

I reflect on Woodstock's abstract cloak of presumed innocence. For the charge of stealing food from St. Clarissa's he's already spent more time in jail than would most adults upon conviction of this petty crime.

Still hoping for a note of reassurance, I suggest, "At least Judge Fetlock stated on the record that Patella's got the burden on the waiver issue." Cuffdon nods: "Yes, we got him there."

When we reach the clinic an associate telephones the only person we can think Patella might have wanted as a witness for his side. After seven rings a gruff voice tumbles from the phone. Its owner gripes he'd been asleep all morning; no one ever asked him to appear in court.

PART THREE: SUPREME VINDICATION

Experience is something you don't need until just after you need it.
— Contemporary Zen

"Don't be nervous," grins my wife Drusilla as I drop a suitcase in the trunk of our Camaro for a seven-hour drive to the state capital. "You're just the first law student to present a case before the Supreme Court. No big deal."

"Of course not, Della," I reply in Perry Mason's voice.

But before I leave the town another problem wriggles out of Woodstock's case. I'm supposed to get his courthouse file certified, so the Supreme Court clerk can register our habeas corpus petition. The file has mysteriously disappeared.

My search for the vanished file leads me to the doorway of the D.A.'s office. "Hi Art, what's up?" Patella chirps as I approach his desk.

I respond to his feigned friendliness. "Lonnie, as a courtesy, I want to tell you I'm appealing Woodstock's bail denial."

I glance down at his desk: "Oh, I see you've got the missing file. The clerk just scoured her office for it. I'll take it to be certified."

When I pick up the folder Patella's face snaps to a scowl. He slams his hand down on the desk. "That file stays right here."

"Sorry, Lonnie," I respond with firmness, "it's the court's, not yours." I tuck it underneath my arm, turn, stride toward the door.

The next five seconds spark an orthopedic miracle: Patella, would-be crippled martyr of a tool-shed bomb, scoots around his wooden desk without assistance from his trademark cane and sprints across the room!

The D.A. whips the file from beneath my arm, clasps it like a football to his side and bellows, "I...said...this...stays...here!"

Legal options gallop through my mind: *Recapture property just ripped from my possession? Rescue public documents? Perform a citizen's arrest for obstructing justice?*

Over these imagined actions bellows my ex-boxer's brain: *Deck the D.A. in his office? Whose career would end with that right hook?!*

Stuffing rage inside futility, I march empty-handed out the door.

Next morning I awake in the state capital, having spent more hours in rehearsal than in bed. By ten a.m. I'm in my shiny old black suit, perched upon a two-inch slab of dark-green courthouse cushion. I press my back against a polished hardwood bench and stare up at the rostrum of the Supreme Court.

To my left sits Professor Bradford Tomlinson, supervising lawyer, patient mentor. (The last few days I've been so combative I fought him over semicolons in our brief.)

Another case begins; the lawyer starts his argument. I excuse myself, search echoing marble corridors for a restroom. As I settle in a metal stall the speaker on a tiled wall announces Woodstock's case!

I rush back to the courtroom, make it by the middle of Tomlinson's introduction: "... an historic first as per this Court's new rule that lets law students practice under supervision in all courts of record in the state."

(Although our case fits inside the wording of their rule, we doubt the justices imagined they would ever see a student in *their* court.)

Chief Justice Lawrence Kerchow notes my tardy entry, nods to me as I stand by my supervisor. I half-bow back. He glances left and right at puzzled colleagues on the bench, fixes me with an Olympian stare, intones, "You may proceed."

I place my outline on the lectern, feel strangely calm, and cast my opening hook: "May it please the Court, I apologize that each of you has only photocopies of the record from my personal file. The prosecutor would not let me get the courthouse file certified."

Three justices leaf through my xeroxed copies in their folders. Two others level frigid stares at me. This student's just implied a law-enforcement lawyer flouted legal ethics and committed crime.

I lay out our case for Woodstock's bail: homeless kid accused of stealing twelve bucks worth of food; juvenile jailed with grown men for several weeks; no date set for trial or a juvenile-waiver hearing; thousand dollar bond denies his right to bail, due process, equal protection of the law. My freedom-lawyer voice is strong, empowered by the feeling that my cause is just.

I pause when Justice Kerchow clears his throat and elevates one massive brow. (Last night Professor Tomlinson warned me, "If a justice stops you with a question, pay close attention. That's when you make or break your case.")

Kerchow's query takes so long a minute staggers by as he constructs a row of verbal boxes, stuffing complex options in each one.

Experience will later show me that good judges think out loud like this, inviting counsel to pounce on any point agree, refute, expand so they can better grasp the case.

But today I'm still a law-school literalist. So I try to organize the boxes as fast as Kerchow's free-association chucks them from his bench. Sweat begins to prickle in my armpits. My mind clambers to an overview of Kerchow's stream-of-consciousness construction yard.

Suddenly I see his whole menagerie of packaged thoughts align behind two gates, one he has expressly labeled "Either," the other he dubbed "Or."

Here it is, I think, *Tomlinson's supreme judicial test, the ultimate law-school exam. Two gates, like that classic tale, "The Lady or the Tiger." One choice will determine win or lose.*

Justice Kerchow finally tacks a question mark on his extended monologue, lifts both massive eyebrows, lets them drop like bamboo blinds.

It's time to stand tall for my client, make good childhood dreams of championing the right. Silence reigns in court. Tomlinson and other lawyers, clerks, stenographers, and spectators lean forward, watch to see which gate the student will select.

In another burst of insight, mental tumblers click in place; the proper choice springs free. Indeed the logic is so tight I can compress it to four words!

I inhale deeply, speak for Woodstock and for freedom, for the law-school clinic and the student-practice rule:

"The latter, your honor."

Air explodes from Kerchow's lips, his square jaw drops, his countenance retreats to puzzlement.

I can't see my answer's only plucked one option from the dozens in his mind. I don't realize so many notions lurk behind his double gates that he can't sort them out!

Unaware of what I've done—or failed to do—one thing's all too clear: My answer didn't wind the clarion of truth.

But Mercy roosts with Logic on the jurist's black-robed shoulders. It prods Kerchow to another question, one that taps against the heart of Woodstock's case: "What if we maintain your client's bail of one-thousand dollars but condition it on personal recognizance?"

Despite hours of prepping arguments, answering scores of likely constitutional queries from the bench, I haven't scrutinized the bail statute. If I had, I'd know that "personal recognizance" would free my client instantly.

So, I stalwartly resist.

"We appreciate your honor's gracious offer of recognizance but Mr. Woodstock can't afford its thousand-dollar price."
I slowly shake my head and add, "Your honor, it might as well be a million for my impoverished client."

Kerchow's tangled brows converge to pup tents; he's stunned by my response. Tomlinson writes fiercely on his legal pad, stretches forward, plops it on my lectern. In large, black, felt-tip letters it yells,

OK — AGREE !

I do.

Five smiles spread across the face of justice. Woodstock is released.

Ever since that day, both in and out of court, when I catch myself constricting life's complexities behind gates labeled *Either/Or,* I hear distant echoes.

One's a voice that earnestly asserts, "The latter, your honor." Another bids me to investigate *all* options til I find the one that says, "Okay—Agree."

THE THANKSGIVING ADDICT

What is justice? — Socrates

That's what my wife Drusilla called him when we finally slammed the doors on our Camaro. By then we were four hours late for a family gathering two snow-drifted state lines down the road.

* * * *

A few weeks earlier I'd graduated law school, won a two-year fellowship from Georgetown, the chance to earn a master's degree in criminal justice. Dru and I had moved our meager worldly goods to Washington, D.C.

I'd passed the D.C. bar exam, bought a dark blue pin-stripped suit, and proudly signed up to defend impoverished people charged with crime.

I was passing through arraignment court the day before our country's yearly holocaust for turkeys when I heard, "Mr. Campbell, I'll assign you to this case of heroin distribution."

Surprised, I turned around; the bass voice boomed from Judge Gaston Pizanno.

"But, your honor, I'm scheduled to leave the District in an hour for Thanksgiving with my family."

"Looks like you'll be a little late," he growled.

I glanced at a cadre of attorneys clustered near the judge's bench, each one eager to accept this case I'd tried to dodge. They glared at me, that scholar-activist from Georgetown with nerve enough to protest as he ripped food from their jaws.

Most of them were "Fifth Streeters," so-called from their dingy offices on a street beside the courthouse. Bottom-feeders of the D.C. Bar, they eked out their living from the troughs of court-paid cases for the indigent accused.

Fifth Streeters usually talked to clients only once—in courthouse lockup—then sat down to bargain pleas with eager prosecutors. They pled nearly all their clients guilty, sometimes ten a day.

These licensed opportunists didn't waste their time investigating facts, finding and preparing witnesses, filing motions, analyzing points of law; forget about a full-blown trial. Like butchers dressing meat, they offered up appointed clients as conditions precedent to paydays bankrolled by the court.

Instead of satchels crammed with motions, pleadings, client files, many only clutched a bulging date-book, interleafed with scores of pink-hued court-appointment slips.

Once I asked a Fifth Streeter why he never tried to get his clients out on bail. "Because I know right where they are when they're locked up." I thought, *What you mean is jailed clients can't skip out the day you set to plead them guilty, close your fist around some courthouse dough.*

Court personnel and prosecutors viewed these lawyers as necessities to keep the courthouse throat from choking as it swallowed droves of indigents charged with crime each day.

But above this grim digestive process beat a stark arrhythmia in the heart of many urban courts. Stroke one: ninety percent of all accused could not afford a lawyer. Stroke two: if more than ten percent demanded trial, the judicial process would break down.

My knight-warrior's mind analogized Fifth Streeters to
Auschwitz guards; they smiled reassurance as they
processed each day's load of victims for the Fatherland.
They weren't even spurred to work for the republic's sake
but simply to enlarge their bank accounts. These slick-
talking scavengers betrayed justice and the indigents
they'd sworn to serve.

But like them, that day I couldn't chose who'd be my client.
So Louis Drame became my first appointment, first felony,
first solo case as member of the D.C. Bar.

One count accused him of possessing heroin; the other of
possessing it for sale.

Louis sheathed his five-foot-seven frame inside a hundred-
fifteen pounds of flesh. At twenty-three his handsome face
still flickered with naiveté. Polite and deferential, he
looked me in the eye: "Mr. Campbell, if you can get me
bailed out, I'll do anything you say."

It took two hours to get him freed upon non-money bail (a
budding specialty of mine.) I phoned Louis' relatives and
friends, plus possible employers. I also telephoned my wife
at home, asked if she would call our folks, say we'd be late
for our reunion this Thanksgiving eve.

Then I strode back to court, convinced Judge Pizanno
that my client's ties to the community outweighed his risk
of flight.

As Louis and I walked three blocks to my office at
Georgetown Law, I recalled his promise to do anything I
said. Would he embark with his addiction on the Good
Ship Rehabilitation? I'd help him to enlist and chart his
course; he'd keep entries of his progress in a log, a pocket
notebook to be carried at all times.

At trial we could show how hard he now was fighting to defeat his heroin addiction. Even if found guilty we'd have evidence at sentencing that he would benefit from a nonconfining disposition, that he was making strides to turn his life around.

Louis readily agreed. I phoned a batch of drug programs, got one to accept him; then Louis and I drafted an ambitious plan to help him sail straight. He'd take daily dispensed methadone, report to the bail agency, maintain a paying job, and rejoin his family, wife, and daughter five years old.

About 5:30 Louis shook my hand, thanked me for my help with bail and his ticket on a rehabilitation ship. As Dru and I nosed our Camaro through a snowstorm, only silent courthouse gods knew Louis' ship was sailing toward the Port of Grief.

A month later at preliminary hearing in a federal magistrate's court, two narcotics officers claimed they'd fielded the tip about a suspect's standing on the corner of 14th street, pushing contraband. They said when they approached, Louis tried to swallow two small plastic bags.

Two hefty officers couldn't make anemic Louis spit out the alleged evidence. Yet after he'd been cuffed and thrown into their cruiser—*voila*!—they swore one plastic bag of heroin appeared inside their car, one more on the curb.

Another oddity: both narcs testified it took four officers to bust my skinny client even though he hadn't tried to fight or flee.

On cross-examination I started lobbing loaded questions at the narcs, suggesting they'd economized the truth. Magistrate Margolis interrupted me: "Rephrase, Mr. Campbell, so you won't sound so cynical."

Spectators tittered; the prosecutor donned a mask of disbelief as I argued with Margolis to continue asking baited questions.

"But *why*, counselor?"

"To show my client's bust was just a dropsy case."

"And what is a *dropsy* case?" Margolis asked in mock magisterial ignorance.

I responded, "Where police shake suspects down, can't find any evidence, but drop some contraband to justify their search and make the case."

Margolis slowly shook his head. "All right, counselor, I'll cut you some slack but don't use the extra rope to hang yourself."

In hindsight I believe Margolis let me try to lasso penny answers with five-dollar questions because it was so rare to see appointed counsel struggle to dismiss a drug bust for an indigent.

At preliminary hearings most Fifth Streeters merely listened to the prosecutor's case so they'd clutch some "facts" to throw at clients, convince them they had better cop a plea.

Of course, following this open-court disclosure of my strategy (I should have whispered it at side-bar), both narcotics officers made sure I'd never reach my goal.

While making futile charges at the narcs' stone wall, I glanced behind me, saw the other two arresting cops among courtroom spectators. I cursed myself for failing to exclude them while their buddies testified.

I'd blown the opportunity to call them to the stand without their hearing unrehearsed specifics I'd extracted from their cohorts. I had lost the chance to let one contradict another, drive a fatal stake into their case's credibility.

As expected, Magistrate Margolis found evidence enough to justify my client stand trial in six weeks. Louis and I tramped back to my office, discussed entries in his rehabilitation log, then shook hands and said good-bye.

* * * * *

Another month elapsed, making two that Louis faithfully adhered to our drug-treatment plan.

It seemed a win for all concerned when I convinced the prosecutor to drop drug-traffic charges, Louis to plead guilty to possession, and the judge to place him on probation, conditioned that he stay aboard our self-constructed rehab ship.

That day the victory circle embraced Louis and his wife, his daughter, and his new employer. Of course, like a stalwart Fifth Streeter I'd also spared judge, prosecutor, cops, and courthouse personnel the expense of trial. Taxpayers saved years of would-be prison costs.

* * * * *

A year later, driving on the parkway to another trial, I nearly skidded off the road when WAMU-FM blared breaking news: A man named Louis Drame just stormed through the courthouse where his wife worked as a clerk. He argued with her briefly, drew a thirty-eight revolver, shot her dead.

I gripped the steering wheel to control my shock, repeated lawyer mantras, vainly tried to pilot through a tsunami of guilt.

Like E.R. doctors, court-appointed lawyers can't choose who gets their services. I was duty-bound to do all that I could for anyone entrusted to my care.

The adversary system only works when freedom lawyers tug with vigor on their end of litigation's rope.

I wasn't tossed a crystal ball when I was yoked to Louis' case.

It took years for me to own more than professional responsibility for the part I played in Louis' life, to accept the truth that sometimes I—as all of us—forge crucial links in others' karmic chains.

But did Louis ever ponder from his prison cell an irony my mind can't shake? Had his case been handed to a Fifth Streeter that day before Thanksgiving, no doubt he'd have served some prison time, but not decades in a cage. And at least *one* person's life would not have been destroyed.

THE WEIRD CASE

*In law the right answer usually depends on putting
the right question.* — Felix Frankfurter

What can you do with an unlawful pistol-discharge case
when your client is a marshal who confessed he'd shot his
gun for kicks? In this case the clue to stay alert was
signaled by my client's name: Warren B. Weird.

At 4 a.m. two cruiser cops heard a gunshot, saw a speeding
car, and chased Weird through a "high-crime area," cop code
for most of Washington, D.C. When they stopped and
questioned him he candidly replied he fired at a wall
for fun. They seized him and his smoking gun.

With a potential jail sentence of one year, the accusation
seemed an easy prosecution win, given gunshots, pistol,
and a full confession on the spot.

"It was a stupid thing to do, Mr. Campbell, but it was dark,
and no one was around. I shot inside a vacant lot. I'd been
to a party and just learned my pregnant sister's going to
give her kid my name."

Warren, handsome, slim, well dressed was twenty-nine,
living with his wife and two sons in a deeply mortgaged
home. His prior Air Force record was exemplary, as were
evals as a deputy U.S. Marshal. If found guilty Weird
would lose his job; any jail time would doom his house
and wreck his family.

How could I fulfill my oath to "render vigorous defense"
against a slam-dunk prosecution case? Even swapping
Warren's guilty plea for probation would cost his job,
a prosecution offer he refused to buy.

So I filed my career's first motion to suppress seized
evidence (the gun and statements) in my first non-felony
assignment in D.C. Super Court.

At the suppression hearing I got one officer to concede the gunshots "could have been car backfires." Jumping on this ground for the defense, I argued to Judge Braman there was insufficient legal cause for cops to order Warren from his car with their revolvers drawn.

"Fourth Amendment law is unambiguous," I said. "Your honor must suppress all fruit gathered from an illegally shaken tree."

Judge Braman took a different view. He focused on the fact my client drove a Monte Carlo, red-on-black, plunked that puzzle piece beside "could-be gunshots" in a "high-crime area." No doubt he thought, "This picture conjures crime inside *my* mind!"

His jigsaw puzzle pounded into shape, Braman found sufficient cause for cops to stop, search the car, and seize a warm revolver underneath the driver's seat. Gun and statements could be used at trial.

I held another arrow in my quiver, one whose point I'd crafted in my written motion to suppress: Warren had been handcuffed and interrogated without being read *Miranda* rights.

Now that I'd learned what Braman thought about this case, I chose not to press this point in open court. He would either brush the argument aside and rule my client's statements were spontaneous or declare a U.S. Marshal knows *Miranda* rights from constantly reciting them.

Braman was a law-and-order judge, not inclined to cuddle constitutional defenses. To push this point would undercut our credibility and detract from other arguments I wished to make. Because the issue was preserved to argue on appeal, I'd bring two other matters up while still in Braman's court.

"Since your honor's ruling hinges on what actually occurred that morning, would you issue a bench warrant for a crucial missing witness, the other arresting officer? I summoned him the standard way—leaving a subpoena with his desk sergeant—over a month ago. Last week the sergeant reassured me he'd be here."

Braman raised his chin to the courtroom clerk, who handed up the courthouse file. After flipping through its pages, Braman said, "Too perilous, counselor. Your officer's signature on the return shows he got the subpoena too late for me to issue a warrant now."

In disbelief, I asked myself, *Is justice being mugged or just ignored? Did that sergeant dupe me? When did warrants turn "too perilous" for a judge?*

Still on my feet, I moved to exclude the first cop's testimony. After he had testified, the prosecutor could not tender me his confidential report, as required by D.C. law.

Without this prior version of Warren Weird's arrest, how could I cross-examine the police on details of where, when, how, and why they'd chased my client down, exactly what he'd said?

The officer admitted he'd submitted a report but the prosecutor shrugged his shoulders, whined, "I'm sorry, your honor, it's not in my file."

"Mr. Campbell, I'm inclined to give the prosecutor time to locate the report you say you need. Do you agree to continue this case a week?"

From his chair beside me Warren yanked my sleeve. His forehead in furrows, he whispered, "No, no! My lieutenant said we must resolve this mess as soon as possible!"

I addressed the judge: "Caselaw's absolutely clear, your honor. When a prosecutor can't present the prior written statement of his witness, the court must strike that witness' testimony."

Braman sighed and closed his file: "This is consuming too much time. Take it up with your judge at trial."

Disappointed that we'd lost the motion, I was also angry that the judge first bowed to his asserted "peril," then sidestepped the law that would have made us win.

As the clerk announced another case, I gathered up our papers, thrust them in my briefcase, feeling little hope a trial judge would view the case our way.

I shared these thoughts with Warren, plus the off-chance that we'd win reversal on appeal. Warren sighed, "I don't really have a choice. We've got to take this thing to trial. Lieutenant Dagget said the only way I keep my job is if this charge evaporates."

Weird agreed with me that dispensing with a jury would spare him anti-marshal prejudice and maybe trim a judge's wrath at sentencing for "wasting jurors' time" by insisting that a dead-bang loser case be tried.

A few days later Warren and I rose from polished courtroom chairs as Judge Wendell Thompson climbed four stairs and took his seat to try this case. At a sturdy table next to ours a different prosecutor stood, announced, "Ready for the government."

Then the lawyer spied a note scotch-taped inside his file. He gulped: "Your honor, may I have twenty minutes to find the assistant originally assigned this case?"

"No objection," I replied, to show the jurist, recently appointed from a civil-law career, that despite our reputation criminal lawyers could be civil too.

40

The assistant was not found, nor (as I'd surmised) the officer's report. So I pressed Judge Thompson for the caselaw sanction that Judge Braman had deferred.

But Judge Thompson, who by then had read the court's entire file, seized the arrow of *Miranda* that I hadn't shot in Braman's court. He stared down at the prosecutor: "What about the fact defendant here was questioned on the street before *Miranda* rights were read?"

"But he's a U.S. Marshal," sputtered the prosecutor, "He *knows* his *Miranda* rights!"

The prosecutor nailed the crucial point. It wasn't whether Weird's *Miranda* rights were read but were they *known* and freely *waived*. In honesty I couldn't argue that my client didn't know these rights. Nor could he testify he was coerced to waive them by his fellow law-enforcement officers.

But civil-lawyer Thompson viewed the issue like a man whose crim-law booster shots were shipped from Hollywood: These rights must be *read*. The jurist dropped his voice to register solemnity: "So it's the government's position that the Constitution does not apply to its own marshals?"

The prosecutor froze while consternation flapped three times around his head. His face grew red, searching for escape from this unexpected snare.

"I rule that it *does!*" Judge Thompson roared. "Defendant's statements are suppressed."

The prosecutor sagged and peered into his file: No usable confession, a lost police report, possible car-backfires, and a marshal's service gun. He exhaled loudly, looked up at the judge and said he'd drop the charge.

So this weird allegation disappeared. Warren joyously returned to work and family, leaving me to rearrange Judge Braman's picture puzzle to a larger view of "law."

Braman's reluctance to enforce the missing-statement rule was offset by Judge Thompson's over-reading of *Miranda*. The paradox was that had each held correctly, the result would be the same.

Sometimes freedom lawyers win by simply challenging what looks like overwhelming evidence, insisting on due process before clients get locked up. On such days the adversary system says you win when all you did was keep demanding courts and prosecutors heed the rules.

CUT'S GAUNTLET

PART ONE: PAROLE EXAMINER

The journey of a thousand miles begins
with a broken fan belt and a leaky tire.
—— Contemporary Zen

More than my experiences with any other client, the time I spent with Thomas Lester Cummings showed me what's involved in freedom lawyering. I also learned to do it more effectively. What cosmic destiny let us walk together through a labyrinth of law and life in Washington, D.C.?

After Judge Arnold Long assigned me to his case, I met Cummings in the lockup underneath Superior Court. I reached through the latticed bars to shake his hand. Aged thirty-two, he briefly dipped his shiny shaved head, raised it, and revealed a dazzling smile. I realized his alias "Cut" came from the three-inch scar that grooved his cheek.

Last week an undercover cop claimed Cut had pocketed one fix of heroin for a strung-out childhood friend. The charge? Felonious drug-distribution under the Controlled Substance Act, shortened on court papers, "C.S.A."

Then, strange to say, before Judge Long appointed me to Cummings' second case, the undercover officer had bailed Cut out on personal recognizance.

Cut's second charge was lodged last night, called "U.N.A.": possession sans prescription of a listed drug in the Uniform Narcotics Act. The drug? One tablet of amphetamine (desoxyn) allegedly discovered by the same narcotics cop!

Charge three would make Franz Kafka grin: getting busted for the second charge while on bail for the first. Brought under D.C.'s Bail Reform Act, its docket tag was "B.R.A."

These three charges blinked from pink-tinged duplicates
the courtroom clerk tore off and handed me when
Judge Long assigned me to Cut's case.

Not until I talked with Cut did he disclose the broken fan
belt or—to use his words—"a little problem of parole."
When he'd been addicted to heroin Cut was nailed for
drug-dealing, kicked his habit behind bars, became a model
prisoner, got paroled.

He needed nine more months of street time to complete
parole but only one arrest could ruin this, add years of
backup to the total he now faced.

From this barrage of charges plus revocation of parole,
Cut stared at thirty-five more years behind stone walls
whose tops were garnished with barbed wire.

Not appointed to defend him on parole, I volunteered so
we could mount a unified defense. Despite his right to
different counsel and my disclosure that I'd practiced
less than six months in D.C., Cut instantly agreed.

I thought, *At least I'll prepare his cases more than some
court-appointed flunky from Fifth Street—and Cut must
know about those guys. But don't I seem to him like just
another Fifth Street scallywag?*

Then, before we launched our lengthy journey, I heard
hissing from a leaky tire. "Oh yes, Mr. Campbell, I forgot
to tell you. My parole examination is set for ten o'clock
tomorrow morning."

I stopped writing on my legal pad, stared into his eyes.
Damn! I thought, *How can I possibly dig out, vet, and
strategize all necessary facts and law by then? Is this your
test to gauge how well I play forensic games? If so,
you're gambling with three decades of your life.*

"That's not much time to get prepared," I said with a level voice. "I'll see what I can do."

It took forty minutes to complete our interview. Using classic where-when-what-who-why's, I filled eight pages of a legal pad with details of his two arrests: Where had he been walking? Exactly when had cops appeared? What had each one said? Who else had been present? Why did he think they targeted him?

Halfway through our interview, Cut shook his head and smiled. "Man, you take more notes than any lawyer I've ever seen."

Again I held his gaze: "Mr. Cummings, I want *all* the facts. More than cops and prosecutors have. That gives us an edge. Now here's an empty legal pad. Take it to your cell tonight and fill it with the history of your life."

"Well, all right," he said, "... but why?"

"First, I want to know you better. Second, it will come in handy down the road if we have to deal with sentencing. Third, it gives you something you can do to help your case."

"Right on!" Cut exclaimed. "I've got me a *real* lawyer. Man, we're going to celebrate when you knock down these bogus beefs!"

For three seconds I looked at him without expression. Then I smiled, swung my open palm toward his. As our hands smacked, I said, "Make sure the jail knows they've got to bus you to our hearing in the morning."

I walked to my office wondering, *Is this guy a wacko or for real? Or someone in between—urging me beyond my depth, so he can later claim he was denied effective counsel?*

Above my head three sparrows argued in a scraggly sycamore. I thought, *One thing's sure: Cut's upbeat attitude would have bolstered spirits at the Alamo. Just as well. It feels like we're standing on the parapet of that beleaguered fort, facing overwhelming odds.*

The next few hours saw me scrabble through the stacks of Georgetown Law School's library. (This was in the days when mice still chewed on books instead of clicking searchers through a maze of law transformed to ones and zeros.) I unearthed a good critique on parole revocation law hidden in the footnotes of a student article.

I gleaned an overview of how tomorrow's hearing should proceed, plus constitutional arguments I could raise if opportune. Knowing now what evidence was relevant, my jitters over being unprepared reined to a focused trot. I sketched our case's spine inside my mind, then hit the streets to search for flesh to clap on an emerging skeleton.

I tracked down police reports of both arrests, then interviewed Cut's colleagues, seeking those who'd witness to his character and reputation on the job.

Cut worked at Pride Incorporated, a nonprofit program aimed at rehabilitating inner-city youth from sundry drug addictions.

Though most co-workers could not afford to lose a half-day's pay to testify, everyone I spoke to brimmed with praise for Cut's integrity, industry, and devotion to Pride's cause. My initial skepticism was being elbowed out by new respect for this unusual man.

Next morning Cut and I stood side by side before the gun-grey desk of parole examiner Thelma Bloomsey. My right hand held a yellow pad of notes; my other grasped three letters touting Cummings' stellar character.

We left our only witness pacing in the hall outside the hearing room. The man's charisma seemed compressed inside the hallway's institution green, a corridor without a single window, painting, poster, plaque, or photograph.

Ms. Bloomsey pushed two buttons on her tape recorder, introduced our case and personnel. The fact she'd make a record triggered me to open with my constitutional points.

In essence they said Cut's parole should not be revoked upon his mere arrests; until a court concludes he broke some law, due process must presume he's innocent.

I knew in actuality very few parolees duck revocation after one arrest, and Cummings had been busted twice. So my arguments were merely sewn as seeds for an appeal. *Some day,* I thought, *perhaps I'll get a court to straighten out the "process due" in revocation law.*

Since student-lawyer days I'd learned to soften my approach when raising constitutional points. I assured Ms. Bloomsey that I only mentioned them so Mr. Cummings wouldn't waive his rights by failing to object. "But we know that you need facts, not legal arguments, so you can do your job."

I organized our facts by way of two contentions, both at first blush straining credibility: Cut had not committed any crime, and he remained a model parolee.

To support the first I sketched our view of Cut's arrests: An ambitious narc had nailed him with a bogus bust, then bailed him out so he could claim to find a pill inside Cut's coat. The whole campaign was staged to pressure Cummings into ratting someone out at Pride.

These were incendiary times when standard law-enforcement views rejected grassroots movements to clean up inner-city neighborhoods and rehabilitate drug addicts.

I got a nod of recognition from Ms. Bloomsey when I cited D.C. politics that formed a vital context for our case: Pride's hiring of ex-addicts as drug counselors was highly controversial. Cops believed Pride counselors used their jobs as fronts for dealing drugs.

I conceded to Ms. Bloomsey our position was mere theory at this time, that our evidence would have to wait for trial. But I urged by the same logic Ms. Bloomsey's papers held no "proof" against my client, only allegations from a prosecutor's file. "Nonetheless," I said, "we owed you our explanation *why* these two bizarre arrests occurred."

Turning to my second point, I handed the examiner our letters from Pride's officers; they touted Mr. Cummings' leadership and success with troubled youth.

Then I called our single witness, no less than the elected president of D.C.'s School Board, the founder and outspoken champion of Pride. He strode into the hearing room like God in an Armani suit.

Thelma Bloomsey straightened in her chair.

The witness layered praise on Cut for being an inspiring model of recovery from drugs. Nine years enslaved to heroin starting at fifteen, the last eight years Cut not only fought off his addiction but persuaded scores of hard-core kids to follow his example, turn their lives around.

Ms. Bloomsey beamed at our loquacious witness, raised her eyebrows, nodded as he ended every sentence. For the first time since she'd pushed the buttons on her tape recorder I thought, *Maybe, possibly, perhaps she'll recommend Cut's reinstatement to parole.*

She did!

Years later D.C. Mayor Marion Barry crashed his rocketing career into a swamp of drugs and politics. Yet through all his trials and detractors he remained a hero to the poor and disenfranchised of our nation's capital.

Outsiders couldn't grasp how Barry prompted such unflagging loyalty. But I understood it well, ever since that day as our sole witness he sat tall, spoke true, helped keep Thomas Cummings on parole.

PART TWO: SUPPRESSION HEARING

Some days you are the windshield;
some days you are the bug.
— Contemporary Zen

Next time I appeared for Cut I learned how easily a defense can crash when splayed on spindly legs. A prosecutor chopped one leg away; a judge hacked off another; bureaucracy, the third. The last I amputated by myself.

Two weeks ago at Cut's arraignment on the charge of holding one illegal pill, a slim prosecutor in a dark blue suit sidled up to me. She gently grasped my elbow, turned us from the litter of Fifth Street lawyers mewling round her courtroom podium.

In dulcet tones she promised to reduce Cut's charges if I'd spare her narcs from testifying next week at his scheduled preliminary hearing.

I consulted Cut, discussed the offer's pros and cons. Since a prelim merely showed that there was evidence enough to hold a trial, its only benefit for us would be the slim chance we'd discover something new about the prosecutor's case. Cut agreed we should accept her offer, waive the hearing. So I did.

Four days later I tracked the prosecutor to her desk inside a warren of cramped cubicles on the courthouse second floor. I asked that she make good our deal.

Her face flared crimson as she shook her head: "I'm sorry, Art, my boss told me on further study of the case I couldn't drop a single count. I didn't know that when the narcotics officer asked me to offer you the deal."

I held her gaze for an extended moment, thinking, *That cop yanked your chain just like he jerked around my client!* But instead of saying anything, I shook my head, turned, and walked away.

What felt like a shin-kick at the time was the sound of one leg snapping under Thomas Cummings' case.

Should I bring this breach of promise to a judge, move to set aside our waiver based upon misrepresentation by an officer of the court? A year before I would have.0 In those days I imagined litigators as modern knights whose armor only came in black or white.

Since then I'd learned most trials were waged in twilight by champions clad in shades of grey. Moreover, Cut kept urging me to be a realist. He often smiled and shook his head at my insistence other lawyers play by rules of chivalry.

So after Cut and I mulled over what to do, I followed his advice. Instead of battling to restore a relatively pointless hearing, I deposited the prosecutor's broken promise as a credit in the courthouse favor bank. Next time we needed something within reach of her discretionary power, she clearly owed us one.

I thought of asking her consent to let Cut out of jail pending resolution of his charges. But I knew the D.C. bail statute said defendants can't be freed on personal recognizance a second time when they'd been busted while released upon non-money bond.

From the outset of this case I'd planned to file a motion to suppress as tainted evidence the pill "found" on my client by the narc. As I'd argued to the parole examiner, the cop might well have planted it to make Cut rat out some suspected pusher in the rehab program where he worked.

Sprouts of my suspicion blossomed when I learned the same narc and his partner lied about another drug-possession bust. Last week under skillful cross-examination by a counsel for defense, one cop contradicted crucial aspects of his colleague's testimony. Indeed the judge who heard their stories was so peeved he ruled they had conspired to convict a citizen with perjury.

I knew clever cops would not step into this trap again. They'd diligently rehearse, conform their stories on the what, where, when, and how of Cut's arrest. But my motion to suppress would also let me fire questions at their "why's," a target I hoped they'd overlook.

Why had they zeroed in on Cut? Why did they think their "confidential tip" was credible? Why did their tipster know exactly when and where my client would be strolling down the street with one pill nesting in the lint of the left pocket of his coat?

The legal basis for my questions was our challenge to the constitutionality of Cut's arrest. Although police bust people everyday, few people realize that each arrest without a warrant is "presumed unconstitutional."

This means police must later prove in court that facts existed at the time which triggered an exception to the Fourth Amendment's dictate that arrests be scrutinized by judges before cops pluck people from their workplace, streets, or homes.

If police cannot establish an exception, *Wong Sun,* a fundamental-freedom case, prohibits any prosecution benefits from the arrest. Branded "fruits of the poisoned tree," they must be thrown out by a judge.

In our case the narcs had to prove their confidential tipster was "reliable," that he'd furnished good tips in the past. I could question both cops on this point, try to show their bust a set up or a sham.

By quirk of an evolving set of D.C. court reforms, all drug-*possession* issues (e.g., the tablet of desoxyn) were tried in Superior Court. Three blocks away Federal Court resolved drug-*distribution* matters. (viz, Cut's charge of dealing one fix of heroin.) This meant I'd defend Cut's two drug charges in two different courts.

Today a judge in D.C. Super Court would hear our motion to suppress the pill. I strode into the courtroom acting much more confident than I felt.

Slapping down my leather briefcase on the table for defense, I zipped it open and spread out my notes. Glancing nonchalantly to my right, I saw both plain-clothed officers confer in earnest whispers with the prosecutor; the latter wore a worried look.

Questions leapt into my mind: *Did they just inform him that their busts were faked to make Cut turn state's evidence? Will prosecutor ethics—plus due-process law— prompt him to disclose this fact, or even drop the charge? One can always hope....*

Nothing near these fantasies ensued when both narcs shuffled to the front row of the courtroom and sat down. The prosecutor merely turned to me and asked, "Are you ready for the clerk to call our judge?"

"Sure am," I answered boldly, "but the hearing has to wait until your marshals bring my client from the jail."

Before Cut came, a wobble in our case's second leg appeared. The back door to the courtroom yawned and Tinley Nutsall heaved his corpulence up four steps behind the judge's bench.

Cut and I just lost the courthouse lottery, the random pick of jurists who resolved pretrial motions in Superior Court. We'd drawn a classic egotist from bobbing lines of black-robed bigots stretching back to England's birth.

Looking like a portrait of Sam Johnson in his waning years, Nutsall tried to cloak his ignorance with arrogance: "*Wong Sun?* Who's *Wong Sun*?!" he blustered at my mention of controlling precedent.

Next I heard the sound of bureaucratic gnawing on the third leg of our case. A red bubble on the courtroom phone lit up. A clerk snatched the receiver, listened fifteen seconds, then said, "Call us every twenty minutes. Tell us what you've learned."

The clerk announced that court and jail personnel had failed to jibe their bussing lists. Cut, who should be sitting next to me, was still inside his cell across the town.

For the next two hours U.S. Marshals phoned our courtroom clerk, who dutifully relayed their bureauspeak: "Mr. Cummings continues unretrieved inside the system."

Nutsall fumed at the delay, already angry he must hold a full-blown hearing to suppress one tablet of desoxyn instead of getting to pontificate before an audience of citizens trapped inside his jury box.

Time slouched down the corridor as Nutsall handled other matters and I chose to sit outside his courtroom with two witnesses for the defense. From different places on the street each had seen Cut's second bust, would testify the taller narc had thrust a hand in his own pocket just before he shoved it into Cut's.

Plying them with sweet rolls, coffee, words of confidence, I repeated how we needed both their points of view, urged them not to bail on their chance to bring the truth into this case.

Finally Cut arrived from jail.

Before the start of testimony I invoked the "rule on witnesses." Reluctantly Nutsall observed this rule by ordering one narc from the courtroom while his colleague testified.

When I dug for "whys" I hoped to catch the first one unprepared and wanted to be sure the other wasn't listening. Otherwise the second could repeat whatever ad-libs stammered from his partner's lips.

It wasn't long before I realized these veteran officers had anticipated all my angles of attack. By the time both narcs had finished testifying they'd drawn a warp and woof of words so tight I couldn't snag a single errant thread.

Indeed, I thought they did too good a job. Each used the other's phrases so repeatedly their song sang more of long rehearsal than the truth.

Once the second cop precisely parroted a dozen of his partner's words. I turned and raised my eyebrows at the judge. Had he heard that clang of artifice? Nutsall nodded back at me in recognition then switched his expression to a leer as if delighting in this dittoed ditty by a narc duet.

Near the close of each man's cross-exam I rolled out a cannon that I thought would blast his credibility. I asked about his testimony in last week's drug-possession case. In response both officers feigned complete amnesia of the fact another judge had ruled they both were perjurers.

Throughout their mimicked lapse of memories all I could do was stand and grind my molars. Not only was I unprepared to prove their former lies in court but I was also helpless to reveal they were lying now about their prior lies.

What crushed this leg of our defense was my ineptitude: I'd failed to procure a transcript of that other lawyer's case!

I still clung to hope Cut's case would clamber from the floor and march to triumph on the backs of our two witnesses.

Rufus Pearl was the first. He'd been walking on the street with Cummings when the cops seized Cut. He testified about the narc magician's slight of hand before he'd thrust his fingers inside Cummings' coat, pulled out the plum of one illicit pill.

Then, despite long preparation in my office—"Keep it simple, tell it straight"—Rufus lurched into embellishment so lavish that he staggered toward the pit of self-incrimination: "I might have handed Mr. Cummings something just before the bust, but it sure wasn't any pill."

Nutsall slammed his gavel on the bench, called a halt to testimony, ruled Rufus needed 5th Amendment counseling from an independent lawyer.

Coaxing half a dozen colleagues in the lawyers' lounge, I finally persuaded one to set foot inside Nutsall's court. He merely whispered into Rufus' ear the essence of my warnings days ago: "Tell the truth but don't say something that could land your butt in jail."

55

When Pearl resumed the witness chair, he prefaced his response to my first question with the idiom "Well, to tell the truth...."

Nutsall smacked his palm against the bench, stopping Rufus in mid-sentence, then asked mockingly, "You mean everything you've said til now was just a lie?"

As shock spilled from Rufus' jaw, Nutsall smiled and slowly scanned the prosecutor's face, the courtroom clerk's, the marshal's, and stenographer's. Submissively each smiled back at this judicial mugging cellophaned in wit.

Cut looked at Nutsall as a lion might regard a toad. I bowed to Rufus: "Sir, would you continue telling us the truth just as I'm sure you have since you first took the stand?"

Rufus labored through the balance of direct and cross-exam. When he stepped down, the jowly jurist raised his chin, declared, "The court won't give his words an ounce of credibility."

I called our second witness to the stand. Leavesley Pound had watched Cut's arrest from a bus stop down the street. He repainted Pearl's picture with much plainer, cleaner strokes.

But dregs of my remaining hope dissolved on Leavesley's cross-exam. Although I'd fully prepped both witnesses, I hadn't tried to iron out the natural wrinkles rising from their different points of view.

Nutsall's pupils danced behind coke-bottle lenses as the prosecutor scratched each variation until Leavesley's testimony seemed to burst into a flare of lies.

On a more pervasive level, from the outset of proceedings another gremlin had been kicking at this case's legs. The night before, I'd given in to fears I might not keep my wits about me as I tried to prove two seasoned cops were lying, then reconstruct the scene with words from Pearl and Pound.

This led me down the classic path of over-preparation. I redug the pitfall of a thousand tyro litigators: penned a detailed script of questions I would use for every witness, theirs and ours.

Today as both sides testified, I thumbed through my pad of twenty scribbled pages, unable to refocus quickly, follow up effectively, or probe new possibilities that came to light.

At the close of testimony, staggering on its wobbly legs, the fall of our defense arrived as no surprise. "Motion to suppress, denied."

Despite the fact that Nutsall seldom granted defense motions, I slumped in my chair and looked dejectedly at Cut. I'd lost our bid to block a single tablet from condemning him at trial, a pill with potency enough to heave him all the way to prison.

What surprised me, though, was Cut's reaction to our loss. He leaned sideways, whispered, "Don't take it personally, Mr. Campbell. No way we could win our motion with this judge."

As the courtroom cleared, Cut and I went over other motions I had planned to file. Two beefy marshals edged toward us; one announced they had to bus Cut back to jail.

Just before they reached us, Cut extended his right fist to me. Looking in his deep brown eyes, I bumped his fist with mine. We hooked thumbs a second, then released and snapped our fingers— a sign of solidarity he taught me years before it discothèqued into a hip cliché.

That evening I drove home with my Camaro speakers at full blast. The sound drowned out my curses heaped on lying cops and prosecutors, biased judges who refused to try, and attorneys like myself who failed to do their best.

PART THREE: PAROLE BOARD

Fill the seats of justice with good men
but not so absolute in goodness
they forget what human frailty is.
— Sir Thomas Talfourd

Cut was dealt a clutch of charges: one felony, two
misdemeanors, one violation of parole. But he also drew
an ace I'd played and planned to use again.

Today we'd face a panel of the D.C. Parole Board, knowing
all it had to do was point to one of Cut's arrests to justify
revoking him, send him back to prison for three years.

Last month school-board president Marion Barry testified
on Cut's behalf before the parole examiner. When Barry
stepped down from the witness chair, the examiner
recommended Cut stay on parole.

I'd lead with this ace, then reveal face cards I had found in
Cummings' deck. Two of Cut's co-workers promised to
appear and testify to his good character.

When our case was called, however, not a single witness sat
beside us on the oaken bench outside the hearing room.
"Damn!" I said to Cut, "I should at least have drafted
a petition, got it signed by all those kids you helped."

"That's okay," Cut smiled, my senior by five years and half a
dozen lives. Then with the assurance by which he'd settled
street disputes and talked addicts off of drugs, he added,
"You'll do fine in there."

At the outset of the hearing I sparred with Chairman
Wilburn Ferrel when he asked to change the order of the
topics we'd address. Would I first show my client was a
good risk for parole? Then he'd let me whittle at the
charges facing Cut. Recalling student-lawyer days, I yielded
before I ticked him off.

58

Further research had convinced me to abandon laying down a record for appealing to the courts. Executive discretion of parole boards stretched so wide that judges seldom second-guessed its reach. So whether process "due" or not, Cut's revocation could be based on allegations long before a trial tested them for truth.

I bit my lip when Ferrel mentioned Nelson versus Sard, a local case my research hadn't found. When I confessed my ignorance the chairman's stern face softened. "The case," he said, "will shield Mr. Cummings' words before this board from any later use against him in the courts."

Prior to the hearing Cut and I prepared his testimony. I pelted him with tricky questions members of the board might ask. We worked on his consistency and clarity, planned him as our final witness; that would let him answer any issues that arose from other witnesses.

Ferrel's citing *Nelson* warned me we might have to lead with Cummings' testimony as we waited for our other witnesses to show. A thought kept tugging at my mind: *What if they had come, not knowing our case was being heard behind unlabeled doors, shook their heads, and walked away?*

Finding willing witnesses, getting them prepared and present at a hearing, always called for delicate diplomacy, sometimes outright begging. Mentally I kicked myself for not having my investigator drive them here. He would have found the hearing room and made sure they'd wait.

Nonetheless, for twenty minutes Ferrel let me argue facts and logic, build our case that Cut's post-prison life had been exemplary; that charges lodged against him were a setup; that he'd been singled out to finger others where he worked.

"Mr. Chairman, before I ask my client to testify, may I step into the hall and see if any of our witnesses are there? They'll shed a lot of light on Mr. Cummings' character."

Instead of answering, Ferrel leaned first toward one, then the other, member of the board, softly parlayed with both men. Then he straightened from the huddle, smiled broadly, and declared, "That won't be necessary, Mr. Campbell. The Board's decided it will reinstate your client to parole."

Cummings and his lawyer glided from the room on skis of air.

No sooner did we reach the corridor than a would-be witness galloped up to us. "Sorry... I'm so late..." he gasped, "but I took some extra time...to fetch this letter."

I pulled the letter from an unsealed envelope and scanned its single page. Apologizing to the Board for not appearing personally, Marion Barry had spread unstinting praise for Cut on his official letterhead.

Reading over my shoulder, Cut grabbed me in a bear hug. Suddenly I felt how much I longed to get this good man on the street again.

That evening the *Washington Post* phoned for details why, despite three pending charges, the Board continued Cut's parole. I omitted Marion Barry's name. Instead I mentioned Cut's accomplishments and leadership, reminding the reporter that any adverse "evidence" was just a prosecutor's claim.

Then I asked the journalist a freedom-lawyer question: "Don't you agree...sometimes when defendants get their story heard, our system comes out right?"

60

PART FOUR: DISCOVERY HEARING

*Trial judges search for truth; appellate judges
search for error.* — Legal Maxim

The charge that Cut had palmed one fix of heroin for
a needy friend would be tried in Federal Court.

It would be my first excursion there; also first discovery
motion and first hearing before Judge Thomas Flannery,
former United States Attorney for the District of Columbia.

In prior attempts to deal with allegations facing Cut, I
wasn't sure if I'd persuaded the parole examiner and her
board that all my client's charges stemmed from sham
arrests by two ambitious narcs.

Perhaps it was just Marion Barry's backing that convinced
parole officials not to order instant revocation, instead leave
it to the courts to sort things out.

But I'd clearly failed to sell our defense theory to a law-and-
order judge in D.C. Super Court. Now I'd get two other
tries, first before a federal judge then a jury of Cut's peers.

My briefcase didn't overflow with hope. It was, however,
crammed with pretrial motions. One was to discover what
evidence the prosecutor planned to use to prove his
heroin-palming case. Another was to make the narcs reveal
the informant they said led to Cut's arrest. The third was
to suppress the tinfoil packet one narc claimed he'd seized
from Cut.

Today the hearing for discovery would launch our federal
defense; I'd done some heavy lifting to prepare.

In civil litigation each side's evidence marched from one attorney's office to the next. Habitually disclosed were names of everyone with knowledge of the facts, their addresses, statements, records, including those of cops. Potential witnesses got deposed in privacy for hours before the trial began. Thus seldom was a civil lawyer shocked in court by hidden evidence.

But judges handling criminal cases seemed obsessed by fear that witnesses would be intimidated or evidence corrupted if defendants knew too much of what lurked in their adversary's file. Such jurists minimized the items prosecutors must disclose before a trial.

That let crafty prosecutors stash grenades of evidence to lob against defendants—"Surprise!"—in trials with liberty and lives at stake, not just cash and real estate.

As a freedom lawyer I wanted to create a record to appeal the unfairness of this double standard in civil versus criminal trials.

Filing a four-page list of items to discover from the prosecutor, I knew defendants rarely got the things I sought. Besides demanding everything the other side would show the jury, I asked for names and home addresses of all this case's narcs, informants, witnesses, plus transcripts of related phone taps, photos, bugs, pen registers, et cetera.

Stapled to my list were thirteen pages of authority and arguments. I'd adapted them from memos Addie Bowman lent me in his defense of Vietnam War protestors, the once-celebrated "Harrisburg Seven."

This morning Cut was timely bussed from jail to court. He sat beside me, studying his copy of our motion, nodding every time he turned a page.

Cut's calmness was contagious, which today I'd sorely need. Last night I'd decided to present our complex motion without script or outline, just a checklist of key points penciled on one page.

Our hearing started with an unexpected turn in Cut's direction: The prosecutor failed to appear in court. As ten minutes ambled by, Judge Flannery, a solemn man with deep-set eyes and greying hair, became so irked he granted by default each one of my discovery requests!

But before a marshal came to handcuff Cut and bus him back to jail, a breathless prosecutor, told by phone of Flannery's expansive ruling, rushed in.

Gripping both sides of the podium to anchor his surging lungs, he bleated, "Your honor... I'm so sorry.... I forgot the hearing was today!"

With flush-faced sincerity he begged the judge to reconsider his unprecedented ruling. I knew Flannery possessed complete discretion in such circumstance; I had no basis to appeal his change of mind.

I watched Flannery's scowl slowly morph to satisfaction that he'd scared respect into the guy. The prosecutor's candor was so rare in court, odds were the jurist would reward it by reversing his decree.

Before he did I seized a tiny moral hummock for our side: "We don't want justice to depend upon a prosecutor's memory slip. Defense has no objection to your honor's reconsideration."

At the time I didn't realize my small concession set the scene for higher stakes that would arise before this strong-willed judge.

Today it only let me plow the ground for an appeal of discovery's double-standard. The prosecutor and I made a thorough record as we thrashed out every item I'd demanded he divulge.

The outcome was predictable: Judge Flannery allowed discovery only of the standard things, disclosed at standard times.

PART FIVE: DAY OF TRIAL

Sometimes ther's nae better way to kill a dragon then to charge right up to it and shove a spear down its throat.
— *Michael Murphy*

Defense attorneys frequently face lying cops in witness chairs, know their perjury still sways jurors more than words from "criminal" defendants. Cop shops try to justify their torturing of truth by claiming, "All defendants lie. We're just balancing the scales."

What's rare for the defense are times when it can prove a cop is lying on the stand.

Early in Cut's case we smelled setup by an overreaching narc. After claiming Cut was pushing heroin, he got Cummings out on bail, then arrested him again, allegedly for one pill of amphetamine "found" in Cut's coat pocket.

We predicted that the narc would pressure Cut, after prosecutors brushed aside all motions from his lawyer, to help them nab a suspect pushing drugs inside the rehab program where Cut worked.

Last week I'd asked my investigator, Collot Bruce, to see if she could pry a statement from this narc, pin down details of his version of events. I wanted copious quotes but told her not to hope the guy would spill the name of his alleged informant for the bust.

Collot returned with seven pages of the narco's words inside her green-lined steno book. Yes, the cop maintained his tipster's anonymity. But he candidly revealed other aspects of his scheme, eager to impress the winsome blonde each time she scooted forward on her chair, tossed him wide-eyed prompts like "Really?" and "Oh, wow!"

Another rare delight for the defense is bringing into court a secret prosecution witness, one so sacred cops claim only they—not even judges signing warrants based upon the person's words—can know his name or whereabouts.

Despite the narc's refusal to divulge his source, Cut and I were fairly sure the man was Evron Comber, Cummings' strung-out friend and would-be user of this case's single fix of heroin. Smiling at the irony, I subpoenaed Comber as our chief witness for the hearing where I'd ask the court to formally unmask the secret agent's face.

Cut was now my veteran client. In my mind the high stakes of his gauntlet fused with my respect for this insightful, patient man.

Repeatedly I'd drawn upon his savvy to appraise key players in our struggle: police, prosecutors, judges, both sides' witnesses. Cut had a canny sense of when self-interest slanted people's views, when some words were fear-concealing bluster, others hazy but still true.

Assessing one important witness for our side, Cut said, "Rufus used to be a big-time singer but his years inside a bottle make him nervous when he's sober. That's why he overstated things last week before Judge Nutsall. Next time, before you put him on the stand, look him in the eye, let him know how much we need his words without the jive, how he's got to carry justice into court. And make sure you feed him first."

I studied Cut's extraordinary empathy. I also sipped from his deep well of confidence that no matter how bleak things appeared, somehow they'd turn out right.

Of course he furthered his own interests, reaching out to help a rookie lawyer labor with half-sharpened litigation tools. And well he might; our campaign would determine if he'd spend his next three decades in a cage.

Last week, after ruling on our motion for discovery, Judge Flannery had calendared a brace of hearings, followed by Cut's jury trial, all running back-to-back until complete.

As I climbed the courthouse steps I swung my briefcase jauntily in hopes its rhythm would dispel my gnawing sense of doom.

Today's first hearing would resolve our motion to suppress as evidence that fix of heroin allegedly concealed for Cut's friend. The basis of the motion was our challenge to the previous reliability of the narc's informant.

This was the secret someone who, the narc had claimed, knew exactly what Cut looked like, what he would be wearing, where he would be walking at a designated time, and precisely what was in the left-front pocket of his army-surplus coat.

To heed Fourth Amendment law, the prosecutor had to prove this tipster was reliable—in narcolese "that he was a confidential source who had given truthful information in the past."

At our second scheduled hearing I would argue that the search for truth demanded cops divulge the name and whereabouts of this mysterious source. The court should call him to the witness stand, subject him to time-honored tests for truth. Only after cross-examination could Judge Flannery determine his reliability.

After that would come Cut's jury trial. All three would be firsts for me in Federal Court.

Today both Cummings and the prosecutor arrived at court on time. Judge Flannery strode to the bench, his gait radiating power. The clerk announced our motion to suppress.

The prosecutor's major witness was the narc who'd busted Cut. From caselaw on this subject, all the narc need do to squelch our motion was swear his confidential source had given trusty info in the past, recite a few particulars, then describe how he had seized the forecast tinfoil pack.

It may have been the narc was scared such testimony would reveal clues about the I.D. of his tipster, or that his source possessed a paltry history of reliability. Perhaps there was no tip at all, just the narco's plan to frame my client, squeeze him til he ratted someone out.

For whatever reason, the narcotics officer took the stand and oath, then falsified his testimony, contradicting what he'd told Collot.

"Cross examine, counselor?" asked the judge?

I stood, faced the officer, centering my weight above both feet, then fired an impeachment cannonball across his bow: "Isn't it a fact last week you told Ms. Collot Bruce a different story?"

Puzzlement cascaded down the narco's face. He blanched and stammered, "Well, I think...I don't believe..."

I watched his thoughts stampede along the well worn hall of liars chased by prior contradictions til he stumbled through a common exit: He feigned a memory lapse.

With wide-open eyes he pivoted to face the judge and claimed he totally forgot what he had said last week as Collot jotted down his boasts inside her spiral book.

Then his ice-blue irises blazed at me as if I'd sprouted horns. With self-righteous dignity he blustered, "Mr. Campbell, your investigator lied to me! Said she worked for the D.A. I would have told her nothing if I'd known she'd come from you!"

I affected nonchalance but the narc's response struck like a right hook in my ribs. I paused to ask myself, *Could Flannery see through this guy's attempt to gig me with a trick that recently appeared in D.C. news, behavior that could cost a lawyer's license?*

Then a perfect question struck me. I stiff-armed fear for my career, saying to myself, *Deal with his slander later. Right now strike—the iron's hot!*

"If you thought Ms. Bruce worked for the prosecutor, you would have told her the truth, right?"

"Of course!" he snapped, then grasped what he just said and tried to squelch the sunrise shooting up his neck.

Flannery gave Dame Justice time to straighten out her skirts. Arching one snarled silver brow he slammed his hammer on the bench, announced, "This hearing is adjourned until tomorrow, ten a.m.!"

* * * * *

That night I phoned the prosecutor, convinced him that Collot and I were not so stupid as to masquerade as agents of the government. I added that I held a dozen lethal quotes in Collot's notes, warned him I could prove his case was riddled with rank perjury.

Next day in court I heard another rare confession from a prosecutor, although cloaked in altruistic terms. At the outset of proceedings he addressed the court: "Your honor, I've just learned my officer made some errors on the stand in order to protect his confidential source. Before Mr. Campbell continues cross-examination may I recall this witness, let him clear a few things up?"

"No objection from defense," I chimed, "We'd love to hear the truth."

The narc resumed the witness stand, reversed himself on several, but not all, the statements he had made about his confidential source and why he'd set Cut Cummings in his sights.

When my turn came to question him again, there still remained some crucial uncorrected points. Before exposing other gouges in the face of truth, I offered him a final chance to ply some plastic surgery.

"Having just admitted perjury before this court, are there any other places in your story where you falsified your testimony?"

He slowly panned his gaze across the ceiling, dropped it to the courtroom door behind which I knew Collot sat beside her notebook full of quotes. He grimaced, "No, that's all."

I repeated four more lies he'd sworn to yesterday, asked if he still claimed that they were true. He glared at me and answered, "Yes, that's the way it was."

"No more questions for this witness," I declared, shooting him a Perry Mason smile. I asked the bailiff to invite Collot Bruce to the stand.

But as she paused inside the courtroom door, I thought, *Why not try a long shot?* I tossed my legal pad on counsel table, frowned first at the prosecutor, then the judge.

"Your honor, at this time defense requests you grant its motion to suppress. The prosecution shouldn't be allowed to build its case against a citizen on mounds of perjured testimony."

Judge Flannery drilled his gaze into the back of the retreating narc, then slammed his walnut gavel on the bench: "Granted!" he declared.

Stunned at this response, I thought, *Good God, this monster of a case is vulnerable!*

Although my last request was totally unplanned, instinct urged me, *Seize the moment, thrust into the dragon's heart!* I dropped my voice to steady it: "Defense moves to dismiss all charges against Mr. Cummings."

"On what grounds, counselor?" asked the judge, his face keen with interest.

My brain raced for words, some rationale to reinforce the signal from my gut. "Inability to prosecute. With no valid evidence or testimony the prosecution has no case."

The jurist raised the brass-rimmed hammer to his chin, held it for three seconds, banged it down. "All charges are dismissed!" Judge Flannery rose from his leather chair, right-faced, marched from court.

This was it. Five months climbing Everest with a toothpick and a trowel. Now against all odds we stood on top! In momentary disbelief, Cut and I stared at each other. Then he grabbed me, wrenched me off the ground, and whooped.

As we waited for the clerk to authorize Cut's release from custody, I wondered, *What made Flannery so willing to dismiss all charges? Was he outraged by the lying narc? Did he doubt a jury would believe the prosecutor's witness once I drenched him with his prior lies? Or did the jurist seize his chance to duck tomorrow's headlines touting "POLICE PERJURY" in his court?*

Upon reflection I'd choose "all of the above."

When we reached the courthouse corridor Cut stepped to the public phone booth, placed a hurried call. Then he turned to me, declared, "Counselor, it's time to celebrate. You got some time?"

"Hell, I've got the whole damn day! You just screwed me out of my first jury trial."

He beamed, "Hey, man, you just saved me thirty-five whole years!"

＊ ＊ ＊ ＊ ＊

For months after our ordeal Cut helped me find elusive witnesses for other clients. We covered inner-city bars and alleys that without him I'd have never left alive. He vouched for me with folks afraid to talk, persuading them to sign their statements, testify in court.

Once I bailed him on a vicious-sounding charge: "A.D.W. — Assault with a Deadly Weapon: Shod Foot." A guy had jumped him on the street. Cut karate-kicked him to the ground. Via statements from eyewitnesses and discussions with police, I got the case dismissed.

As far as I could tell, Cut never shoved another needle in his arm, although he hated his parole-mandated methadone. "That stuff enslaves you too," he said. "By the way," he added, "ever wonder why urbanites call reefer *weed* but suburbanites say *grass?*"

Two years after victory in Flannery's court, a week before Cut's birthday, I telephoned his home. Cut's mother answered. I asked where he was, perhaps we all could celebrate?

"He's dead," she said. "Some woman knifed him in a bar because he wouldn't change a song he'd set up in the jukebox."

Then she politely lied: "I tried to call you for his funeral. It was real nice. Dressed him in his favorite suit. You know, the tan one with those black pin stripes?"

I gripped the phone in shock, tried to tell her what her son had meant to me: a man of wisdom, wit, compassion, strength, and leadership...my friend.

She swallowed down a sob: "Yes...he was very special. We'll all miss him."

I hung up; my eyes brimmed with tears. Then I saw Cut Cummings smiling at me through the mist:"Cheer up, Mr. Campbell, we sure had some high old times."

I recalled that glorious day Judge Flannery dismissed all charges. Joined by Cut's attractive fiancée, we joked and laughed and hugged from noon til eight at night, left our staggered footprints between half a dozen bars.

As years go by I realize how much I gained from our relationship. More than improving advocacy skills, I learned how a man maintains integrity despite adversity and laces moral strength with practicality.

Our comradely struggles had dissolved the customary barriers between appointed clients and their lawyers: different types of social power, different colored collars, different shades of skin.

Ask me who my all-time favorite client was, I'll always answer, "Cut."

DISORDERLY, D.C. STYLE

Before you criticize someone, you should walk a mile
in his shoes. That way when you criticize him,
you're a mile away and have his shoes.
— Contemporary Zen

Like many lawyers who excelled in school by taking reams of notes, I felt nervous speaking off-the-cuff. In court I used my other strengths—fact investigation, logic, legal research —in attempts to minimize this handicap. Meanwhile I searched for ways to overcome it.

During trials and hearings my brain felt maxed out having to remember rules of evidence, procedure, statutes, cases, and the facts that bore upon my client's case.

Amidst the clash of adversarial swords and dictates from the bench, I didn't trust my mind to conjure cogent arguments and questions on the spot. So I penned lengthy scripts, attempting to anticipate all legal points and questions I'd need next day in court.

But running Cummings' gauntlet boosted my experience and confidence. While on my feet I began believing I'd recall all necessary facts and law. This untangled me from stapled pages, let me deal more strategically with somersaults of evidence, those jukes that pop up in every trial, unforeseen the night before when crafting detailed scripts.

Although I wasn't ready to conduct entire trials on the wing, by the end of Cummings' cases I had found a zone between no notes at all and clumsy manuscripts.

I prepared for legal arguments by jotting cardinal points on 3 X 5-inch notecards, one argument per card. When on my feet I forced myself to speak extemporaneously, now and then glancing at the notecard in my hand so I'd not miss a point.

But I hadn't solved the problem of effective questioning of witnesses; breakthrough in that zone would take a few more weeks.

I was getting used to the card-prompting process when Tyrone Sarver strutted through my life. Tyrone and his buddy Lester Grey had been busted for disorderly when they dissed two cops arresting someone passed out on the street.

Lester had forfeited $50 collateral at the station house, amounting to a guilty plea and fine. Tyrone had said, "To hell with that. I'll take my case to court."

Next day, from a notice posted by the courthouse clerk, I saw I'd been appointed to defend Tyrone. Ten minutes before Judge Arnold Woffard gaveled chaos into order in arraignment court, I called out Sarver's name.

Barely past his teens, Tyrone swaggered up to me in superfly attire: flared-cuff trousers, blousy ginger shirt, shoes with pointed toes. His every word and gesture oozed disdain for court-appointed lawyers and "this dumb harassment beef."

Lester volunteered to serve as Tyrone's witness. However, for the next two weeks both men ignored my telephoned reminders to stop by my office and prepare for duty in the witness chair.

On trial day the calendaring judge dispatched us to the courtroom of Judge Waldo Witherspoon. He once lived in my home state; knew my father. Two months ago his secretary sacrificed an evening of her life to baby-sit my screeching infant son.

Before the prosecutor called the first of two cop witnesses, Witherspoon okayed my oral motion that the second officer remain outside the courtroom while his colleague testified. Nonetheless both cop's versions of the facts came across convincingly alike.

74

During their arrest of an unconscious drunk my client
nearly sparked a riot among bystanders. He'd shouted at
the men in blue, cursed them, jerked at one cop's arm.

My cross-exam of each was quick. Except for digging out
the fact no riot had materialized, there were no gems to
mine for Tyrone Sarver.

I rejected what I'd seen too often practiced as a tactic by
defense. Regardless of the type of case, some lawyers
retraced every tittle of direct exam in hopes that one cop's
recall would diverge from what he'd testified before
or what a cohort said.

With relatively simple facts surrounding a spontaneous
event, I figured this approach would only give each officer
a chance to reinforce the prosecutor's case.

After each officer conceded that no riot had ensued, I scanned
the prosecutor's incident report. Finding no discrepancies,
I announced, "No further questions for this witness."

When the prosecution rested (does the defense ever rest?)
I called Lester to the stand. He laid counter-testimony on
so thick I saw Judge Witherspoon's gaze begin to climb
the wall in disbelief: "Tyrone was *always* courteous, *never*
swore, never *touched* an officer."

Tyrone's testimony followed, swabbing golden gloss across
his colleague's rosy narrative.

At the close of evidence I urged Witherspoon to drop his
gavel somewhere in between the two extremes of cops'
and defense views of what transpired on the street.
Anywhere his hammer struck, I claimed, would clang
with reasonable doubt.

Witherspoon reacted to my argument with a countenance of quartz. When I sat down my mind flashed to another D.C. judge who, after two martinis at a party, whispered, "Mr. Campbell, when it comes down to believing cops or citizens, I always choose the cops."

Today the prosecutor tweaked this common bias, asking Witherspoon "which side had the most to gain by twisting truth?" Accordingly, the judge spent little time in summing up the case and finding that "the real facts" all pointed to my client's guilt.

Tyrone's first conviction resulted in a ten-buck fine (forty dollars less than Lester's forfeited collateral). But it yielded me three firsts in D.C. Super Court: first completed trial, first bench trial, and (no trumpets, please) first guilty verdict.

Then a strange event occurred. As I frowned, shoving notecards in the pocket of my briefcase, Tyrone jumped up from his chair and pumped my arm. "Mr. Campbell, it's okay. I knew we'd lose this case. But thank you, counselor, for giving me the chance to save my face."

I forced a smile, held his handclasp, slowly shook my head. The part of me that hated losing cursed him silently: *You jerk! If you and Lester would have prepped your testimony with me, toned it down to plausibility, you might have saved more than your face!*

Suddenly Cut Cummings' spirit shoved an elbow in my ribs: "Art, you'd appreciate what went down on the street and in the court today if you had walked a while in Tyrone Sarver's shoes."

SETTING UP THE ROLL

Lawyers spend a great deal of their time
shoveling smoke. — O.W. Holmes, Jr.

As soon as I completed Sarver's trial I walked down the courthouse corridor, told Judge McIntyre's clerk I was ready for preliminary hearing in Mustav Gerry's case.

I took a seat at counsel table, waiting for the clerk to page my client from the witness lounge. After leafing through the notecards for his case, I sat back and pondered my career.

I'd been representing D.C. indigents for nearly seven months, learning something useful every day about the law, life, or myself. My former knightly earnestness had been tempered with alloys of urban irony. When people asked me how I spent my days, I now *grinned* replying, "Oh, you didn't know? I defend the unjustly accused."

Did I view Mustav Gerry's case that way? Mustav faced a prosecutor's two-tined fork; either point could pitch him in a prison cell. He was charged with both attempted and completed burglary of the same establishment.

Three weeks earlier at 2 a.m., alarms had jazzed a cop-shop monitor. Perhaps a break-in was occurring at the local liquor store. A flock of night shift officers swooped down on Mustav and three friends emerging from a lightless alley.

The alley sprawled behind the back of the alarming liquor store. Cop logic: "These guys must have done the store."

This left a challenge for the prosecutor: All four men were walking empty-handed. But she knew she didn't need to prove that any merchandise was taken, just that the group broke in with an *intent* to steal. The tripped alarm was evidence a door was breached; that only left intent for her to prove.

So she thrust a shovel in her barrel full of prosecution smoke and tossed attempted burg on the defendants. No doubt she expected that the extra charge would spark a deal. If one pled guilty to attempt, she'd drop completed burglary for that guy.

The court assigned each man a lawyer to avoid conflict-of-interest in the case. How so? Prosecution deals with multiple defendants normally require bargainees to testify against their friends. Whoever bought the deal would have to swear the others harbored an intent to steal.

However, for the last three weeks each alley ambler stuck to his not-guilty plea.

Today the prosecutor still seemed unconcerned. At preliminary hearing she only needed to parade some circumstantial evidence before a judge to keep the case alive for later trial. "By then," she must have figured, "surely one will roll to dodge the prison risk."

* * * * *

Mustav and his friends strolled into court; each shook hands with me. All wore clean pressed clothes and recently had graced a barber's chair. Soon we were joined by their defense attorneys.

This would be my first prelim in D.C. Super Court, first case before Judge McIntyre, and first time trying to coordinate a strategy with three other lawyers.

We arranged for me to sit at the end of counsel table so I'd be last to swing my axe of cross-examination. That would let me drive my blade a little deeper into aspects other counsel brought to light. I could also cut away potential chips that might surprise us at a trial down the road.

Two policemen built the prosecutor's case with neatly interlocking testimony. No counsel uttered an objection; we'd agreed to make our goal discovery, not a kill.

When I rose to cross-examine, I aimed mainly at the specter of a prosecutor's later gliding into court with hidden-camera footage, fingerprints, eyewitnesses, phone-tips, stolen property, incriminating statements, and the like.

I'd come across this tactic from a book by F. Lee Bailey; he called it "closing doors." Each cop categorically denied existence of the evidence I itemized.

But police had strategies as well. Because witnesses at prelims can offer hearsay testimony, both cops juggled what they'd seen themselves with supposed observations by three fellow officers.

Moreover, they conflated all these views, so it would be impossible to pin the real speaker down at trial. Inwardly I groaned: *Damn! I should have subpoenaed all the cops, made each one commit to what he heard and saw.*

The hearing ended with Judge McIntyre's echoing a phrase at least three centuries old: "I find sufficient evidence to bind defendants over for a trial." (Actually, each remained "unbound," having easily made bail.)

I knew the prosecutor couldn't win at trial unless one client rolled and testified convincingly against his friends. Now each had a lawyer who would or should protect him from what paradoxically are labeled "law enforcement tools."

Each day cops and prosecutors seat citizens inside small rooms without a window, just one desk and chair. Standing over them, they yell or whisper, "Swear to what we want to hear, and in return we'll drop or won't press charges or we'll ask the judge to cut your time."

Conning and coercion are the common currency of these back-room servants of our law. Courts have even let cops lie about the evidence to trick or scare their targets into nodding at desired testimony.

Ever since I'd hung a law degree upon my wall I'd been proud to echo words of Percy Foreman, distinguished Texas freedom lawyer. Referring to the U.S. Constitution, he proclaimed, "Of *course* I'm in law enforcement—I enforce the law against the *state*."

But if Foreman or yours truly even *hinted* that a person swear to something in return for our pledge not to press a charge, we'd be nailed for extortion, blackmail, subornation of perjury, compounding of a felony, obstruction of justice—or all of the above.

So much for our adversary system's highly touted level playing-field. In the name of equal opportunity, do I think defense attorneys should be allowed to wield these prosecution tongs? Absolutely not! Tricked and coerced statements have no place in courtrooms of America.

Given my distaste for truth-corrupting tactics, it may sound strange that before Mustav Gerry and his friends were called to trial, I withdrew from the defense and became a prosecutor.

"What the hell!" you may well say. I'll tell you what and why inside the final pages of this narrative.

JUVENILE CHARGED WITH RAPE

*The sword of truth, the only sword that heals
as it cuts.* — William Sloan Coffin

Did George Glandell, an unarmed, skinny kid of fifteen
rape a robust woman, twenty-two years old? That was
the underlying question of my first trial in juvenile court.

Proceedings stretched across four days. Two were held
before one judge to find what evidence was constitutional.
Another judge consumed two more to weigh that evidence,
determine if the charge was true.

Co-counsel for defense was Myrna Raeder. She argued for
pretrial discovery of all the prosecutor's evidence. Then
she brought a motion to suppress George's lineup I.D.
by the complaining witness.

Myrna won the right to copies of most items we had
sought: police and medical reports, lab tests, lineup photos,
etc. She also punched holes in the I.D.'s fairness, but
couldn't get it thrown out as too botched to pass
due-process scrutiny.

Throughout these proceedings we faced an inexperienced
prosecutor, short of stature, wide of girth, long on feistiness.
He tried to mask his ignorance of caselaw, trial tactics, even
common sense by simply fighting every move we made.
Heedless that he often muddied uncontested waters, he
needlessly prolonged the trial, irked both judges in the case.

Minor points sparked major flares between this bluster bag
and me. Only one thing we agreed upon: George's status
was a "juvenile." No claim was made that he was so mature
or the alleged offense so aggravated that he must be tried
as an adult.

Perhaps, I thought, *this was because the prosecutor, an assistant D.C. Corporation Counsel, would otherwise lose jurisdiction of this case and the chance to boost his resume with having tried a charge of rape.*

My job was to quash two statements yanked from George, the first extracted after cops had grilled him for five hours without a lawyer or a parent. Judge Fauntleroy didn't need much nudging to declare this statement was coerced, thus inadmissible at trial.

But cops told George to utter these same words twenty minutes later after they had led George's mother to their interrogation room and set her down beside her son. I called that second statement "tainted fruit plucked from the first confession's twisted tree."

We wanted Ms. Glandell to take the stand, describe how the policemen acted their charade of good-bad cop; how they instructed George to say in front of mom what they had made him say before.

But as soon as Ms. Glandell took the oath and eased into the witness seat, her hands seized its arms as if she'd just been strapped to an electric chair.

Oh no! I thought, *just like her son, she has a terror of authority and what might happen if her words don't please. And now she's got to speak in court! I should have prepped her better for the jolt most folks feel when they first touch a witness chair.*

Ms. Glandell stammered out her name and home address. With frequent halts to catch her breath she said she'd been a single mother for nine years, raising George and his younger brother.

I directed her attention to the date when she'd been summoned to the precinct for her son. Abruptly she broke down in tears.

"Ms. Glandell," I asked with all the reassurance I could teleport, "perhaps you have a tissue or a hanky in your purse? Please, take all the time you need to straighten out your thoughts. This must be very difficult for you."

But when she recovered well enough to speak, she could only stumble through terse answers to my questions. She omitted nearly all the crucial details she'd recounted in my office.

I decided not to push her fragile focus any further and sat down. I thought, *George can testify to these particulars although they won't be as persuasive, coming from the lips of the accused.*

Smelling blood, the prosecutor rose, stalked towards the witness chair. "You never, ever saw an officer strike your son or yell at him, did you?" he sneered.

What remained of her composure shattered. Sobbing now, she shook her head. "Mrs. Glandell," the judge politely chided, "you've got to answer using words, so the court reporter here can take them down."

"Yes, sir, judge, your honor.... I'll try."

The prosecutor asked a few more questions, got halting one-word answers, then he also quit.

Perhaps it dawned on him that Ms. Glandell's unexpected breakdown was buttressing our case. Just as in the courtroom, her shaky presence at the precinct would not have shielded her son from overbearing cops nor inspired him to blossom forth with truth.

I called George to the stand to add specifics that I'd failed to elicit from his mom. But after he'd seen mother lose it, he tumbled down the mine of sudden memory loss. He testified he couldn't recall a single detail that surrounded the extraction of his second narrative.

Indeed, on cross-examination by the prosecutor, George became so flustered he denied he'd even signed the first, five-hour statement when cops peeled it from their grille!

Silently I cursed myself: *Why wasn't I more realistic about how traumatic this would be? Why didn't I prepare them better, warn them how they might react in court? How they had to lay aside their fears and make our picture clear? Had I so soon forgotten Cummings' lessons about empathy?*

Lacking solid testimony on which to base a ruling for defense, the judge could not accept my argument that the second statement had been poisoned by the first.

Instead, Judge Fauntleroy concluded mom's appearance at the precinct, yoked to her alleged words—"Son, just tell the truth"—had cleansed George's second statement of its taint. "It won't be suppressed," he ruled.

* * * * *

Norma Johnson was assigned as George's judge for our non-jury trial. Reputedly a tough school marm before she took to law, one pretrial ruling made it clear she would be firmly in command.

A week before our trial I'd served a police desk sergeant with a subpoena duces tecum ("under penalty of law, you must bring designated things to court"). It demanded copies of case records from the precinct where the rape allegedly occurred.

We needed other leads or suspects the detectives had unearthed, all witness statements, and if complainant said things inconsistent with the claims she later made.

As soon as Johnson took the bench, I asked the sergeant to be called from where he waited in the hall. He shuffled into court and took the stand without a single document. When I asked where the court's required papers were, he shot the judge a look of pained annoyance, claimed the records "couldn't all be found by trial date."

"Mr. Campbell," said the judge, "you should have given the police more than a week to comply with your request. No, ... sit down, counselor. Let's move on with other pretrial matters."

More than a week! I thought in disbelief, *To copy half a dozen sheets of paper?* My face flushed from frustration with the judge and anger at the cop but I obeyed and took my seat.

Of course, the crucial trial witness was the woman who'd claimed sexual assault. Blonde, in her mid-twenties, she marched down the courtroom aisle, settled her full-bodied torso in the witness chair.

She swore a man had raped her, that he weighed about 170, wore a smallish Afro, bore no facial scars, and looked to be nineteen or twenty years of age.

Myrna deftly handled cross-examination. Rather than attack a trauma victim's faulty recall or suggest she harbored bias fueled by shame or rage, Myrna simply asked how positive she was about the man she said had thrown her to the ground and penetrated her. The witness iterated her description, concluding, "Yes, I'm sure that's how he looked."

"That's likely why," I later argued to the judge, "her finger wavered at the lineup when she'd pointed out our client. As you see, your honor, from the lineup photograph George appeared the same as he does now: 127 pounds, large Afro, two facial scars when viewed up close, and fifteen years of age."

Throughout George's trial the prosecutor acted with remarkable consistency, never strayed from knee-jerk opposition to every move I made. Once I held my clipboard out to get a document he was obliged to give me; he tossed the paper on the floor.

Judge Johnson dropped her jaw in disbelief, then raised it to a classic teacher's scowl. "Gentlemen, clean up your acts right now. I won't have playground hijinks in my court."

George took the witness stand again, better prepped to keep his cool, pause to think before he offered a response. My opening question asked him to explain his first forced statement at the precinct.

Johnson slammed her hand against the bench. "You suppressed that, counselor! I'm not supposed to know of its existence!" Her words, of course, revealed that she'd read the courthouse file, already knew.

I replied with equanimity, "We trust your honor won't rely on it as evidence against our client. But I disclosed it so the court can see George's second statement merely parroted the first. That way we hope you'll give the second very little weight."

Johnson propped her chin upon one palm, her grimace slowly simmering to guarded contemplation.

This time George did well explaining how he'd given in to pressure after five hours of browbeating by two cops in their cramped interrogation room.

Next I wanted Ms. Glandell to show how the confession chamber looked, how tired George appeared, how the cops played out their highball-lowball roles to wring the second statement from her son.

From her breakdown at the prior hearing I knew there would be problems keeping Ms. Glandell on track. I'd need to guide her not to skip essential points. In case the judge or prosecutor challenged me on my approach, I'd researched and printed up a memo of authorities to support my use of witness prompts.

Tension started building when Judge Johnson blocked my first two questions aimed to bring key facts to light. Despite the absence of a jury which prompting might influence, my third question triggered fireworks from the bench. "Mr. Campbell," Johnson yelled as if I'd slapped her face, "you know you can't lead your witness in my court!"

"But, your honor,..." I protested.

"Don't argue with me, counselor! Frame your questions properly!"

With that command I couldn't even tender her my memo showing that it's perfectly okay to mention *topics* to a witness on direct, just not feed her *answers*. Angrily I circled "McCormick, *ON EVIDENCE*, Chapter One" on my unused memo. I'd raise this issue later, if I had to, on appeal.

My next maneuver made me want to smack *my* face. I marked as evidence, then showed the judge, George's report card of less than stellar grades. My purpose was to prove he wasn't smart enough to outwit savvy cops; they'd tricked as well as forced him into saying what they wanted for their case.

Former teacher Johnson flipped the card, ran her finger down its lines: "Mr. Campbell, your client got this string of D's from skipping class!"

Then I stumbled on another gaffe. I should have known the District of Columbia's special way of qualifying witnesses to testify about a person's character.

I called George's tenth-grade teacher to the witness stand. Hanson Dubar was a well built man, in mid-thirties and a modest three-piece suit.

I'd planned for him to tell Judge Johnson of my client's school-wide reputation for shy gentleness. This, I'd later argue, minimized the odds that George would sexually assault a stranger; far more likely the assailant had been someone else, the larger, older, unscarred man complainant had described.

It took me two wrong starts—this time with Johnson tossing helpful hints—before I qualified our witness and brought forth his testimony.

In my opinion Myrna saved the day for George on cross examining the prosecution's doctor. She pried a major fact from him: the victim still possessed a hymen, bruised but certainly intact.

It's true the crime of rape includes the slightest penetration, needn't go to hymen depth. But this revelation contradicted what the victim said, condemned her credibility.

End result? The judge found George not guilty as he had been charged but of *attempted* rape.

Trying to absorb this baffling verdict, I asked myself, *Did Judge Johnson's compromise arise from doubts about our client's guilt of anything? Did defense's sword of truth slice only halfway through her shield of constant certainty?*

Having been exposed each day to a parade of citizens, most pleading guilty to some charge, had Johnson lost the hammer that's supposed to pound not-guilty verdicts out of reasonable doubt?

Next month, following juvenile-court "disposition," I asked myself again: *Did her qualms George was the culprit move Judge Johnson to impose the hand-slap consequence of probation for one year?*

A few weeks later I spilled my morning coffee when I came across a story in *The Washington Post*. George's self-righteous prosecutor had been busted on a marijuana charge. Cops said they found a pipe and stash in plain view in his bedroom when they burst into his home, responding to a neighbor's phoned-in call of burglary!

This occurred about the time D.C. prosecutors were scurrying to hide beneath a document they otherwise spent half their time attempting to evade: the U.S. Constitution.

Stuffing their executive branch inside the Separation of Powers Clause, they claimed they could ignore a recent trial-court decree by Judge Giles Warfield.

Warfield ordered that, before they jailed inner-city indigents for possessing pot, prosecutors must sign affidavits that they hadn't smoked the stuff themselves.

I happened to be in Warfield's court the day that story in the *Post* appeared. Before proceedings started on another case, I casually inquired if the judge had read about the busted prosecutor. Warfield quipped, "I sure did. That guy deserves a year in jail for sheer hypocrisy!"

SLOAD'S AND BRONE'S PAROLE

[Sometimes] when you tell the truth,
it's a political act. — Simon Ortiz

To a panel of the D.C. Parole Board, Mssrs. Shore and
Coleman, I may have looked like a conniver or a dupe.

I rose behind their deeply varnished counsel table, told
them I was representing two convicted prisoners for no
fee. I merely stood before them on a spot called
pro bono publico.

* * * * *

My relationship with Marvin Sload and Edward Brone had
started with a phone call. Marvin's parole officer asked if I
could squeeze a little justice from a bureaucratic screw-up.
After he explained, I thought of my successful parole
hearings for Cut Cummings and replied, "I'll see what I
can do."

Marvin Sload had been informed his prison record earned
him full parole but on day one of freedom was abruptly
told this wasn't so. Instead he had to spend each night
for three months locked inside a halfway house.

This news had triggered such a rage in Marvin that halfway-
house officials bound his wrists in steel cuffs, sent him
back to cellblock seventeen. All this occurred two weeks
before I got the phone call.

I drove to Lorton prison, submitted to a search, and sat
inside a multi-person conference room, waiting for my
would-be client to arrive.

.

Edward Brone was also there, talking to a woman I learned later was his wife. When she left he noticed I was clientless and seized the chance to tell me he'd just turned parole-able. Would I also take his case before the board? "I'll pay you, man, as soon as I get out of here."

Although immune to inmate promises to pay, I found myself impressed by Edward's story of reform. I said I'd argue that he be paroled as well.

* * * * *

As I unzipped my leather binder to present their cases to the board, I expressed surprise that neither Sload nor Brone were there to sit beside me. "They'll get a chance to tell their story later," one board member said.

It took thirty minutes to lay out Marvin's case, starting with a statement of my interest in his plight: I was part of the legal system that had let him down.

I argued Marvin's momentary fury was a natural response to switching him from full parole to twelve weeks in a halfway house.

As live witnesses I presented Marvin's parole officer from D.C., then his former Maryland probation officer. Both had dealt with scores of rehabilitation failures. Each proposed, by contrast, Marvin Sload was now ideal for parole.

Then I asked the board to look at Edward's case. A former slave to heroin, he was serving time for carrying a deadly weapon during his addiction days, plus one count of mayhem—biting an attorney's finger! "Surely all of us have felt that urge or more," I said. A smile spread across each panel member's face.

I presented documents, showing rehabilitation from narcotic drugs and his steady progress of reform. I gave the board three letters I'd collected from his family and a businessman who promised to employ him on parole; all, of course, urged his release.

Throughout both clients' cases I wondered why proceedings flowed so smoothly: no objections from the board, no barbed questions, not a single look of skepticism. One member even jotted down the points I emphasized.

However, near the hearing's end I saw the jotter switch to drawing sketches on his legal pad. When I showed interest in his art, the other member chuckled, then informed me chances were another panel would conduct my clients' interviews and ultimately decide each case.

"Why don't you pack what you've just said into a folder for their files?" the artist asked. My stomach tightened to a knot. *Holy bureaucrats!* I thought. *Justice ala piecework— how inefficient and unfair!*

When I later checked, I learned this procedure to be utterly routine. My hearings for Cut Cummings constitutionally required my client sit with me before the panel that resolved his case. That was because his case concerned parole *revocation,* not its *grant.* Behind doors of such distinctions do plump bureau-rats reside.

It took eleven days for me to learn of my two clients' fates. Numerous phone calls finally snagged the news as it shimmied down a prison vine: Lawyer-chomping Edward was denied parole, misled Marvin granted his.

I never got official word, never learned the cause for one man's victory, the other man's defeat, never saw or heard from either Sload or Brone.

Pondering why these clients never got in touch with me, I settled on three possibilities. First, I'd worked pro-bono. People often think a lawyer's worth is gauged by what he's paid; that reasoning makes pro-bono lawyers worth exactly nothing.

Second, some clients think all losses are their counsel's fault, all triumphs merely what they're due. Third, I was "of the system." Maybe Sload and Brone believed I'd get the news before they did; perhaps they even waited word from me.

Sometimes freedom lawyering lends little satisfaction beyond knowing you stood up to power, tried to ply a little justice, simply told the truth.

STOP AND FRISK

*Education is hanging around until
you've caught on.* —Robert Frost

The consolation of mistakes is learning something new. I
learned a lot about judicial power when Judge Giles
Warfield slammed his gavel on the bench, called his
courtroom class to order.

My client Phillip Glasto had been stopped by cops when
he turned from a hot dog stand. They frisked him, found
a pistol in his coat. He blurted, "It was in a truck that I was
cleaning for a friend. I was taking it back to him."

Because this was his first arrest and Phillip held a steady
job, he easily made bail the day before I met him in
arraignment court.

Phillip was a deferential man of middle age. When we
shook hands he seemed to teeter on a log of panic floating
in a swamp of shame.

"Mr. Campbell, they nailed me dead to rights. I suppose
there's nothing you can do." I dropped my voice to what
I hoped would be a reassuring tone. "Mr. Glasto, I'll do
everything I can."

But I thought, *How can I mount a vigorous defense against
a gun-possession charge where the pistol's found inside
the pocket of a client who confesses on the spot?*

I recalled a lawyer adage: *When facts stand against you,
pound the law. When law stands against you, pound the
facts. When both stand against you, pound the podium.*

But against this case's avalanche of adverse facts and law it
wouldn't help to whump the podium. All pretrial motions
would be heard by Giles Warfield, a flamboyant judge
intolerant of any bombast but his own.

On the other hand, Warfield basked in his persona as a civil libertarian. I'd look for ways to sound the fife of the U.S. Constitution.

At that time Fourth Amendment law required cops have reasonable suspicion of some crime afoot before they frisked a citizen who happened to like hot dogs. Without this basis for their acts, nothing seized could be used in court as evidence to lock him up.

Accordingly, I filed a motion to suppress the gun and statements. This would place the burden on a prosecutor's shoulders to prove that reasonable suspicion preceded the arrest of Phillip Glasto.

On motion day Warfield's nasal clerk intoned, "United States versus Phillip Glasto." From a front bench in the courtroom I rose and answered, "Ready for defense." For the umpteenth time I turned and scanned the room of witnesses and spectators; Phillip Glasto was not there!

I'd *assumed* that courthouse clerks would mail Phillip notice of the date they'd set to hold our hearing. "A-S-S-U-M-E," another lawyer cliché chortles, "makes an ASS of U and ME."

Concluding Phillip's absence must have been my fault, I approached the bench, confessed my undersight, asked Warfield to continue Mr. Glasto's hearing til next week.

Warfield propped one elbow on the bench, then cupped his chin inside a pudgy palm. "Counselor, I'll give you a choice. You can proceed today without your client or have his motion to suppress summarily denied."

95

Reluctantly I closed my fist around the former barb of this coercive choice. But as I did I tossed the judge a point "just for the record," a phrase that sometimes smoothed down hackles raised at mention of the U.S. Constitution. "As your honor knows, I'm powerless to waive my client's constitutional right to be present at the likely resolution of his case."

I wasn't sure if I could later wrest reversal from being forced to make this Hobson's choice. But my *earlier* admission (already "on the record") etched silver-platter evidence that Phillip had been denied *another* right, that of "effective counsel" from my failure to inform him of the crucial hearing date.

I didn't know if Warfield caught both constitutional shots I'd fired from my hip. But one thing was clear to everyone in court. From his sudden frown, my words had strongly riled this liberal in black.

A second blunder piggybacked my prior folly into court. Since the prosecutor had to justify all actions of the cops, I a-s-s-u-m-e-d that he'd produce a transcript of the "radio-run," a police-band broadcast cops claimed they had heard before they stopped my client on the street.

Their subsequent report declared the broadcast warned them of "a man concealing a gun." Both cops took the stand, swore Phillip matched the suspect in the radio-run's description. Each also conceded that the run was based on "observations by two unidentified young boys."

The prosecutor didn't have a transcript of the run inside his file. And I'd failed to subpoena it. Thus police recollection of the run's description, its weak basis, even its existence, was unimpeachable.

My third misstep was not knowing of a D.C. case decided years before. No excuse, the prosecutor also never heard of it, nor that it had not been cited in a single later case. (This occurred before the law was digitized, allowing every ruling to be traced by desktop mice.)

What made the case important was that it upheld a prior stop-and-frisk decision by Judge Warfield for the prosecution on facts quite similar to Phillip Glasto's case.

Today Warfield bought the cops' consistent recall of the run, then ruled their stop and frisk were justified as per his prior case. After that my client's sidewalk outburst was spontaneous, so it needn't be Mirandized. Thus Warfield dubbed both gun and statements legal evidence for later trial.

My shoulders slumped as I stuffed papers back inside my briefcase. I'd made pudding-head mistakes, lost the motion, even failed to get my client into court.

Small consolation knowing that today had also been the first time I'd conducted an entire hearing using only marginalia penciled on my copy of the motion to suppress.

What good was this to Phillip? Or that my briefcase also clutched three-dozen notecards summarizing any case I'd need except, of course, the crucial one? The only thing I'd done for him was build a record for appeal.

I thought how Warfield, always tough on lawyers who appeared before his bench, had put me through his jurist's form of third-degree. I'd learned firsthand about assumptions and subpoenas, notices to clients, and one obscure appellate case.

But my schooling wasn't done. Warfield shoved aside his gavel, dismissed courtroom personnel with a backhand wave, crooked his index finger at me: "Counselor, would you care to join me in my chambers?"

Oh, God, I wondered like a schoolboy summoned by the principal. *Will he censure me for not informing Phillip of the hearing, criticize my "for the record" point? Did I screw up in yet another way?*

Inside walnut-paneled chambers Warfield slung his robe onto a coat rack, dropped into a leather couch, clunked two ornate cowboy boots upon a table, motioned me into a wing-backed chair.

"Well, Art, you did okay today with all the law and facts stacked on the prosecutor's side." I eased back in the chair, felt my heart release the bars inside its cage.

He smiled, then continued, "Say, if you could control the facts or law on a case like we just had, which one would you choose?"

"Like a judge," I said respectfully, "of course, I'd choose the law."

"Wrong!" he shouted, slammed both boots on the floor. "Trial judges get reversed each week on law, but facts they find stay put."

I conceded the pragmatic wisdom of this point, then, feeling bold, I asked him how a noted constitutionalist had once made law expanding cops' authority to stop and frisk?

Warfield sighed, stared at his oriental rug, then stretched his face into an impish grin: "In those days I was a hard-ass. Then I met a real lady, settled down, and saw the light."

Next day I returned to Warfield's court, announced I'd found a recent case from the Supreme Court that clearly overturned the basis of his judgment against Phillip. It should also overrule his precedent on stop-and-frisk.

Brandishing a supplemental brief, I gave it to his clerk, who laid it on Judge Warfield's bench. I asked, "In light of this new law, would your honor reconsider Phillip Glasto's case?"

Warfield brushed my brief aside, strangely winked, then stated, "Reconsidered and denied." Suddenly his face grew stormy. He growled, "If you don't like that ruling, Mr. Campbell, I invite you to appeal."

Stunned, I held his gaze three seconds, about-faced with martial precision, and strode out of court.

In the corridor I kicked an errant paper, angry that a judge purporting to be friendly, pro-freedom, or at least pro-fair would not even read my brief. As far as Warfield seemed to care, Phillip Glasto's case was closed and school was out for me.

Then I got it. Warfield meant to spur my freedom-lawyer wrath, hoped that I'd appeal, obliterate the stop-and-frisk mistake he'd made before romance had swung him toward the Bill of Rights.

But before Phillip could appeal, he must be convicted of the crime. That meant I'd have to take a factually hopeless case to trial. Although this was every client's right, doing so would mean subjecting Phillip's sentence to a judge's pique, "because your client wasted courthouse time."

Warfield's need to amputate his old right wing meant Phillip's justice train would have to wait with him for months inside the grey-bar roundhouse til a higher court reversed his precedent on stop-and-frisk.

It was hard for me to buy the fact this would-be constitutionalist would heave a man in jail just to purge his pre-girlfriend precedent.

Later in the day a prosecutor phoned me, promised he would press for minimal incarceration if Phillip pleaded guilty which, of course, would waive appeal.

"What if we plea," I countered, "but conditioned on his *losing* an appeal of my motion to suppress?" The prosecutor answered, "Sorry, can't do that."

No doubt he'd surveyed our dismal options, flashed a tempting plea in hopes we wouldn't jeopardize pro-prosecution precedent by appealing it.

I phoned Phillip, discussed the risks of trial and a long-ball sentence, possible reversal after months pursuing an appeal—all weighed against a guilty plea next week and shortened jail time.

Though our appeal might have "made good freedom law" for other citizens, Phillip wasn't born to wear a martyr's robe. He telephoned me back and said, "Let's take the prosecutor's deal." We did.

I compiled a lengthy memo and exhibits for Phillip's sentencing. It documented his achievements back to high school, his steady work at sundry jobs. I included letters from his neighbors, his employers, and his priest. After validating Phillip's upright life they urged non-incarceration for his first offense.

On the day of sentencing Judge Warfield announced, "Counselor, I've perused your sentence memorandum and it's quite a piece of work. Is there anything you'd like to say before I place your client on probation?" Luckily for Phillip, I kept my mouth shut.

COP ASSAULT OR SIDEWALK JUSTICE?

*The character of every act depends upon
the circumstances in which it is done.*
— O.W. Holmes, Jr.

I'll bet the D.C. scooter cop gagged when a prosecutor
lowered Raleigh Roper's charge from "felonious assault on
cop" to the misdemeanor of "disorderly conduct."

This case began when a lone ranger on his silver scooter
putted up to Raleigh as the latter strolled a sidewalk with
his wife and best friend Max.

"Pour that beer into the gutter!" yelled the officer. "You
know you can't drink beer on public streets!"

Raleigh gave the curb his beer and the cop a dose of First
Amendment rights: "Called me *Honkey muthafucka*," later
testified the officer.

Fireworks began when Mrs. Roper stepped to the
policeman's side and rapped a knuckle tattoo on his
helmet. Scooter hastily dismounted, grabbed the lady's arm,
bounced her off a call box, then against a curbside car.

Raleigh seized the wild gendarme, yoked him in the crook
of his right arm, wrenched Scooter from his wife. Max
leapt between the fuming missus and the struggling cop.

For their restraint and gallantry, Max and Raleigh were
jumped by backup officers, slammed facedown on
the ground.

At trial Scooter swore thirty citizens abruptly streamed
from doorways, swarmed him, "throwing rocks and bottles,
knocked my scooter over, kicked it full of dents."

Swiveling to face the judge, Scooter turned up both his palms and bleated, "All I did was try to bring some law and order to that neighborhood."

The cop's apocalyptic vision—riot, chaos, downfall of the Western World—was undercut by one unchallenged fact: the pack of backup officers busted just two men, Raleigh and his comrade Max.

When Scooter finished testifying on direct, I asked for the version of the incident he'd written for the prosecutor. The lawyer pawed his file in vain.

I invoked the standard D.C. sanction for the prosecution's failure to produce a prior witness statement: "Move to strike the witness' testimony, your honor."

But Judge Ryan Nielson balked. Instead he ruled I either had to waive my client's right to strike or yield a week's continuance for the prosecutor to find his missing document.

Three defense eyewitnesses were sitting in the courtroom, a chancy mark to reach again. So I elected to proceed without the cop's report or stricken testimony.

However, to preserve this issue for appeal, I made this pressured choice the basis of a motion for acquittal at the close of testimony.

Before we reached that point, however, I harvested two blunders sewn before the case was even called for trial.

First, I didn't caution my co-counsel, representing Max, not to cross-examine Scooter on the neighborhood's reaction. "Going there," I should have warned, "will blunt the theme of self-restraint by our two clients. Just aim at some strategic spots."

Instead, Max's counsel plunged in blindly, reexamined every detail of the fifteen-minute fracas. Of course Scooter seized this chance to splash more color on his self-portrait as General Custer at The Little Big Horn.

Second, I had failed to insist our witnesses meet beforehand in my office. They needed to rehearse how they'd depict the incident, state things simply, resist the prosecutor's bait on cross-examination barbs.

But non-rehearsal was the only flaw arising from a venture that began with Raleigh's case—one that was a turning point for me in future trials.

* * * * *

Let me sketch some background here.

The last few weeks I'd grown increasingly relaxed inside a courtroom. Yet I kept searching for a more effective way to handle the direct- and cross-exam of witnesses.

At one extreme I'd penned lengthy scripts of Q's and A's on legal pads. At the other end I'd jotted one-word prompts on margins of my pleadings. But for Raleigh Roper's case I tried a new approach.

Two weeks before the trial I asked my assistant, law-student Shelton Williams, to find all willing witnesses, synopsize what each one had seen and heard, including their discrepancies.

I gave him a sheaf of notecards; on each one I'd jotted down in cryptic form a question I might ask in court. Would he summarize each witness' answer to that question on the flip side of the card?

When Shelton later handed back the cards, I chose the ones I'd use, arranged their most effective order and ringed them in a mini binder. At trial I planned to hold the binder in one hand, flip cards with the other and know what answers to expect from every person called.

The binder also organized two other clumps of cards; one set was cites to statutes, caselaw, and selected lines from Bartlett's quotes. The other set continued a procedure I'd been using for the last few weeks: key points for each argument expected to arise.

I had to trust supporting sentences for each card would march from barracks of my consciousness like loyal soldiers through distraction, opposition, nervousness, and sweat.

On trial day Shelton chauffeured our three witnesses to court, sat with them on the courtroom's butt-shined pews. When I arrived he introduced me to a woman and two men, each in freshly laundered clothes, ironed with the pride of working-class Americans determined to see justice done.

* * * * *

My witness' answers to notecard questions wove a lucid verbal tapestry. It revealed Raleigh's vain attempt to save his wife from Scooter's unexpected violence.

But, not having prepped these witnesses inside my office, they were snagged by cross-examination. The prosecutor's taloned questions made our image of two crime-preventing citizens begin to fray.

Hoping I could make repairs on redirect, I flipped to unused notecards in my binder. Asking half a dozen extra questions, I wove our picture back in only slightly tattered form.

Utilizing cards this way completely changed the way I'd handle future witnesses. Instead of being handcuffed to a lengthy script, I could cluster cards around strategic points, rearrange their order when new patterns emerged, save the rest for unforeseen contingencies.

To my relief supporting words flowed from my lips each time I rose to speak. Once when I sat down I thought, *For years you longed to be a freedom lawyer, wondering when you'd master basic skills. Today you feel almost comfortable in court!*

This virgin use of cards became the first time I'd examined every witness on direct and cross without one objection sustained by the judge.

To top it off, when all the evidence was in, all words and motions said and done, Judge Neilson ruled we'd won.

Afterwards I wondered if the jurist feared reversal on appeal for not striking Scooter's testimony. Or perhaps the gap between the prosecution's version and my client's yawned with too much doubt.

But I like to think Judge Neilson took a broader view of freedom law—and let justice rest the way events transpired on the street.

BANK ROBBERY

People who make atmosphere are rulers.
Atmosphere is the principal device of rule
as well as the chief product of it.
   —W.D. Norwood, Jr.

Percy ("Pretty Boy") Floyd takes the prize for most polite,
soft-spoken client I have known. Taped to my notes, his
fading photo from the *WASHINGTON POST* still beams
like the face of a Tibetan monk.

But behind that serenity lived a man of sudden violence.
He had been convicted at sixteen of murder-during-robbery
and later of escape from his "secure" reformatory.

When we met he faced a catalogue of federal charges
stemming from the robbery of a bank whose guard was
killed exchanging gunfire with a three-man gang.

Lois Goodman, appointed to defend him, asked me if I'd
like to second-chair. "Sure," I said, eager to observe her
non-confrontive style, how it converted hostile witnesses,
coaxed cooperation out of judges, cops, and prosecutors.

My assignment was to research and present a pretrial
motion to suppress all I.D.s of Floyd. It would be my first
such motion and first hearing before Judge William Bryant
in his cathedral-ceilinged court.

Research couldn't find a knockout precedent on any of
three grounds our facts made us stand upon. But I culled
persuasive *dicta* ("words") from cases that supported all
my major points. Combining these, I hoped, would nudge
the judge to drop his gavel on our side.

My initial point was crafted from what at first seemed like a
crushing fact: After cops and F.B.I. responded to the bank's
alarm, one teller yelled throughout the lobby, "I know the
guy who robbed us—it was Percy Floyd!"

106

We didn't seek suppression of that statement. Instead we'd leave the *source* of that surprising outburst—a loose-lipped cop who once had busted Floyd—to detonate at trial. It would anchor our defense of was-Percy-being-framed?

But the teller blared this statement in the face of other witnesses, riddling their brains with bias. No wonder they had fingered Percy's photo from a six-pack of selected mugshots, then at a lineup pointed out the guy who matched this photograph.

I argued that, beginning with the teller's prejudicial cry, due process barred all prosecution use of Percy Floyd I.D.s by photograph, by lineup, and eyewitnesses in court.

I made my motion's second point the F.B.I.'s refusal to provide us with all witnesses' descriptions of the gunmen who'd burst through the front doors of the bank.

I claimed our constitutionally required presence at Floyd's lineup had been pointless since the F.B.I. deprived us of the means to make it fair. How could we tell if suspects close to these descriptions stood in line beside our client?

My third point targeted an unfair aspect of all lineups in D.C. Police allowed their officers and the F.B.I. to observe proceedings but ejected our investigator from the lineup room.

Police stopped the only defense witness who could testify to jurors how slow or wobbly each I.D. appeared, whom else tellers scrutinized, how many seconds passed before each person settled on a choice.

Of course Lois and I had been present at the lineup and observed these things, but if we took the stand as Percy's witnesses we'd have to withdraw as his advocates.

I filed this three-pronged motion to suppress, stapled to a
lengthy memorandum of authorities. Next I argued orally
in open court, trying to persuade the judge to rule for
the defense.

From the outset of our hearing I was treated to Bill Bryant's
rare judicial equanimity. One of America's few jurists with
a background in criminal defense, his demeanor was
distinctly Lincolnesque.

As I expounded each point in my written motion, Bryant
leaned back in his swivel chair, then heaved forward,
stroked his chin and asked me searching questions,
making sure he understood defense's point of view.

I felt hopeful when Bryant decried the teller's blurting out
our client's name, berated the denial of non-Percy Floyd
descriptions, and chastised D.C. cops for ejecting our
investigator from the lineup room.

But Bryant challenged me to prove admission of our client's
various I.D.s would be so prejudicial as to shatter Percy's
fair-trial rights. I bit my lip for not preparing more for
Bryant's bottom-line concern.

I had figured, when he weighed our facts, their cumulative
prejudice would be self-evident. *Res ipsa loquitur:* the
thing speaks for itself. Indeed, each case cited in my memo
had found prejudice from one type of error—just not
enough to K.O. that particular conviction. By contrast, our
case bristled with three different types of taint.

Bryant's gentle prodding on this point backed me to the
courtroom wall. I snatched a hypothetical from its carved-
wood scenes of toiling laborers: "Suppose witnesses had
claimed the robber was a giant but they I.D.'d a midget at
the lineup. If counsel didn't know they'd be looking for
a giant, we couldn't put one in the line, much less
understand enough to tell the jury why these witnesses
seemed so uncertain or surprised."

"Yes," said Bryant, "I see *potential* prejudice from conduct of the teller, F.B.I., and the police. But your client's not a giant or a midget, so I don't see how it ruined *this* I.D."

At hearing's close the judge conceded that my arguments for prejudice disturbed him but not enough to rule that Percy's constitutional rights had been or would be vaporized.

I sat down, angry at myself for thinking prejudicial facts would speak up for themselves. *That's what you're here to do!* my conscience growled. I turned to Percy, raised my eyebrows, sighed. From his chair beside me Percy nodded enigmatically.

Taking stock, I thought, *At least I built a solid record for appeal.* As a personal victory, I'd argued facts and law for twenty minutes at the hearing's start, ten minutes at its close, all without support of scripts or even notecard prompts.

It had been a daring move for me to step away from notes. Though I was intimate with every detail of our case, I still harbored doubts my brain would hand down useful sentences through swirling rounds of arguments.

But once again words came. In fact, I revisited that realm of calmness I once felt behind an outline months ago before the Supreme Court.

Despite rejecting all my law and logic in the case of Percy Floyd, Judge Bryant tops my list of thoughtful, patient jurists before whom I've appeared.

Lois brought a brilliant motion, presented over several days, to quash Floyd's whole indictment. She focused on the system D.C. utilized to locate jurors. The district gathered folks from every race and region of the city, people wearing levis, suits, and collars of all shades. But it failed to net enough *young* folks to constitute a valid cross-section of D.C.

Grand jurors who indicted Percy were pulled from this pool of candidates. So Lois argued that, before his trial started, Percy Floyd had been denied the constitutional right to a grand jury of his peers. He'd lose his right a second time if Bryant let trial jurors emerge from this pool.

Lois reinforced her claim with a satchel full of documents. She extracted testimony from the D.C. jury commissioner and employees of the Polk Directory, a database for selling goods and services from which the juror list evolved.

She topped this off with experts in statistics. Their charts and testimony ripped holes in the D.C. system, showed that its reliance on the Polk Directory made it clearly biased against finding inner-city youth.

Judge Bryant wouldn't grant her motion to dismiss (which would have jeopardized a thousand past and pending cases in D.C.). But his extraordinary patience, reinforced by Goodman's charm, let Lois build a thorough record for appeal.

Months later, spurred by Lois Goodman's evidence, the commissioner changed the way the District filled its jury lists; new pools swelled with younger citizens.

Percy's wait for trial dragged on several weeks while he languished in a jail cell. Why did his loyal counsel not object?

Because our brazen escapee with prior unserved sentences could never make the street on bail. And bank tellers' memories—even fused by prejudice—had been known to fade with passing time.

By the morning Bryant finally gaveled Percy's trial to order, I'd withdrawn from his defense and joined a prosecution team.

Although my switch was planned for weeks, the day I said good-bye to Floyd he held my gaze with his compelling stare. "Don't worry, Percy. Your secrets are all safe with me. I won't even practice in the federal courthouse. I'll be three blocks away in D.C. Super Court.

"I'll accept your word on that," he said.

* * * * *

One day during Percy's trial I dropped by Bryant's court. I wanted to say Hi to Floyd and watch Lois ply her skills before a jury of non-Percy peers.

When Bryant called a recess I pushed back the swinging wooden rail—crossed the bar—approached defense's table where Floyd sat, his hands calmly folded on a legal pad.

He looked up, smiled, thanked me for my former service, then declared, "The government is lucky to have such a good lawyer on its side."

Taken by surprise—compliments are rare from court-appointed clients—the only thing I thought to do was clasp his right hand inside both of mine and mutter, "Thank you, man."

Defendants seldom win bank-robbery trials with multiple I.D.s by cocksure witnesses. Percy was convicted on all counts. It didn't help defense's side when jurors learned he'd been arrested with a pre-marked twenty-dollar bill from the assailed bank!

One of my assignments as a budding prosecutor in D.C. Super Court was to placate fire-breathing jurist, Horace L. Bachover. The judge had raised a jury-composition issue on behalf of an accused and then directed defense counsel to file all necessary papers in support.

I leafed through a copy of the filed pleadings and voluminous exhibits. Except for its title page, the package was a photocopy of Goodman's jury-system challenge on behalf of Percy Floyd.

BEDLAM IN AND OUT OF COURT

A closed mouth gathers no foot.
— Contemporary Zen

Sometimes freedom lawyers have to stand their ground
before a tyrant judge and hope the jurist's unchecked
arrogance will blast some error in the record for appeal.
Standing ground can even win a point or two when self-
righteous judges think it was the prosecutor who provoked
their royal wrath.

This case began when Denese Raber, six years old, claimed
Barton Blazelle and his roommate Ruckles Larson stole a
stereo from her home. When? She said, "Sometime after
midnight" on an autumn morning in D.C.

The problem was she told no one at the time, not her baby-
sitter nor two other grown-ups in the house, none
of whom heard what she thought was breaking glass.

Denese allegedly informed her mother of these things
when Mom came home at 3 a.m. Mrs. Raber stormed two
blocks down the street and pounded both her fists on
Barton's door.

She accused him of the theft, dared him let her look inside
his home. Barton stepped back, let her in.

Mrs. Raber couldn't locate any loot. But for reasons that
remain unclear she freaked, grabbed a kitchen knife, chased
Barton' girlfriend through the house.

Police eventually arrived and quelled the scene. They
asked Blazelle and Larson to ride with them to Mrs. Raber's
place. Would they mind if her daughter took a look at
them? Both men, in their early twenties, readily complied.

Denese rubbed sleep from her tired eyes, declared these men were not the burglars she had seen. Barton and his friend trudged chilly streets back home.

Two hours later, nearly dawn, police arrived once more at Barton's door. "We need to be completely sure you aren't the guys we want. Will you go back a second time?" Both men agreed and dressed again.

This time Denese hid behind her mother, refused to say a word. So her father and one cop escorted her upstairs. When the trio trooped back down, police handcuffed Barton and his roommate, charged them with grand larceny and burglary.

Later that same morning Superior Court assigned me to defend Blazelle. After verifying facts about his job, his fixed address and solid family ties, I got him released on a thousand dollars' bail. I didn't realize he'd be my final client before I moved my chair across the courtroom to the prosecution's side.

I filed a motion to suppress all evidence of Denese's pre-sunrise I.D. and declare her too impressionable to testify at trial. I claimed both Denese and her I.D. were "inherently unreliable."

Of all D.C. precedent that supported showup I.D.s, the longest stretch was ninety minutes after the alleged offense. Denese's epiphany occurred six hours afterward.

Pat Wynn, a public defender, stood as Larson's counsel when we appeared before Judge Giles Warfield, noted, inter alia, for launching verbal pyrotechnics from the bench. He'd conduct our hearing to suppress.

That day beneath his robes Warfield rode an angry tiger into court. The jurist snarled curt directions, snapped at any hesitation, sometimes slapped down lawyer inquiries before they reached their question marks.

He barred Denese from entering the courtroom until he'd ordered Larson and Blazelle to sit behind the rail among three-dozen spectators. He didn't want defendants' presence at their lawyers' table to reinforce what he allowed "just might be" her inadmissible I.D.

I liked Warfield's leanings, his creative move, but objected vigorously to what he next proposed: that Denese wander through the courtroom, see if she could point out Blazelle and his friend.

Warfield raised his voice a dozen decibels: "Mr. Campbell, do you mean to stand there pompously and tell me what I cannot do in my own court?"

"Of course not, your honor," I tranquilly replied, "but for all the reasons set forth in my motion she'd be looking for the same men cops brought to her house, the ones both parents told her were the bad guys."

During this debate the chief prosecutor, whom I'd noticed standing in the back of court, marched down the aisle and stepped inside the bar. He surprised me by supporting my objection to Judge Warfield's plan of hide-and-seek.

Warfield roared, "All counsel in this case approach the bench!" Four attorneys—two prosecutors, two for the defense—walked forward, stopping just beneath the judge's elevated desk. Its surface gleamed about the level of our chins.

Without warning, Warfield seized a heavy law book, partly slammed it, partly threw it, on his bench. The tome slid down the polished oak, coming to a halt three inches from the chief's astonished face!

Silence fluttered to the floor.

Warfield must have realized he'd topped his *sua sponte* mark for courtroom melodrama. Hastily he shoveled words into the void and half-reversed himself: Defendants would stay hidden among spectators but Denese would not be asked to search them out.

For the remainder of the hearing Warfield scowled but kept his temper on a leash. After Denese and other prosecution witnesses testified, he ruled the six-year-old was competent to take the stand at trial, adding with a glower, "...if there *is* a trial."

Then he puzzled me along with other lawyers who had flocked to court in hopes of seeing more judicial tirades. He declared Denese's I.D. inadmissible not from precedent or prejudice but because it hatched from hearsay.

As soon as I could grasp this novel way to grant my motion to suppress, I scrambled to my feet: "Your honor..."

The chain on Warfield's patience broke. He yelled, "I thought I told you earlier to keep your big mouth shut!"

"I merely want to ask the Court, in light of all its rulings, to reduce my client's bail from $1000 to ten percent of same."

"Granted, now get out!"

Scooping papers toward my briefcase's mouth, I saw I had sweated through the armpits of my best courtroom suit. I thought, *At least it lasted long enough to weather Warfield's storm, win this motion, set Barton's case along the path of probable dismissal.*

One more surprise awaited me. As I turned to leave, I glimpsed my wife Drusilla's million-dollar smile. First time she had watched me work in court. What a day to choose!

* * * * *

That Friday night I lay in bed inviting sleep and thinking of my hours in the tiger's den, winning just by standing firm. I replayed Warfield's diatribes, smiled at the jurist's bowling caselaw down the bench.

Then doubts about the future started climbing up my spine. On Monday I would turn from criminal defense and join the prosecution's team.

My fellowship at Georgetown offered me the chance to practice as a Special Assistant U.S. Attorney in D.C., a premier prosecution job.

For weeks I'd tried convincing others (and myself) of benefits to a freedom-law career from this opportunity. I'd learn prosecution strategies, and strengthen courtroom skills by trying cases that required me to prove all crucial facts beyond a reasonable doubt. Plus I'd enhance my credibility with ex-prosecutor judges (which meant most jurists in D.C.)

Now in bed I stared at ceiling shadows, wondered, *Can I honestly switch sides, prosecute the poor and powerless, those I'd studied law to serve?* I recalled my office colleagues sniping, "Traitor! Turncoat!" not entirely in jest.

Mixed metaphors began to stomp a cakewalk through my brain: *Have you mothballed your integrity, dropped your moral compass, mounted mere ambition, sold out to the enemy?*

Those epithets had also pelted me the last few weeks. They'd been flung by legal-aid attorneys, other freedom lawyers, advocates of civil rights—in short, by nearly all my D.C. friends.

Would my sense of justice become twisted by the heady power to decide each day which people only have their knuckles rapped, who get instant freedom, who must face a trial, fine, imprisonment, or death?

117

I'd seen this happen countless times to prosecutors, blindly spurred to "punish" or to "win their case" regardless of the truth, due-process, or societal costs.

What would happen to the kid who all his life had dreamed of championing the rights that those with power usually try to crush or brush aside: the rights of indigents, political protestors, dropouts and minorities, those with different life-styles, new beliefs, or unfamiliar gods?

Could I take what I had learned, the courtroom skills I had acquired, and turn them on the folks I'd always deemed my real clients? Was it *possible* to strive for justice from the other side? In short, could a prosecutor also practice freedom law?

One way to find out. In two days I'd seize the chance not often offered to attorneys steeped in criminal defense. I'd see firsthand if justice really needed two sides placing weights upon her scales. Next time I walked into court I'd take the prosecution's side.

AUTHOR BIOGRAPHY

Art Campbell was born in Brooklyn, raised in Appalachia, and scholarshipped to Harvard and Georgetown Universities. Prior to earning his law degrees, he was a road-maintenance worker, janitor, boxer, rugby player, and professional musician. He then became a trial lawyer for and against the government in Washington, D.C. Campbell's poetry has won various prizes and been published in literary magazines and anthologies throughout the United States. Married to the novelist Drusilla Campbell, he now teaches at California Western School of Law in San Diego and trains horses in Lakeside, California.

If you'd like to obtain *Trial & Error Volume II: For the Prosecution*, please contact the author via email — acampbell@cwsl.edu.

BOOKS FROM POETIC MATRIX PRESS

News of the Day
Poems of the Times by John
ISBN 978-09789597-3-9 $16.00

The Unequivocality of a Rose
a poem by Joel Netsky
ISBN 978-09789597-1-5 $15.00

In A Dress Made Of Butterflies
poems by Sandra Lee Stillwell
ISBN 978-0-9789597-0-8 $15.00

Of One and Many Worlds
Buddhist poems by Rayn Roberts
ISBN 0-9714003-9-3 $15.00

Nature Journal with John Muir
edited by Bonnie Johanna Gisel
ISBN 0-9714003-7-7, hc $20.00
ISBN 0-9714003-5-0, pb $16.00

The Lost Pilgrimage Poems
by Joseph D. Milosch
ISBN 0-9714003-8-5 $15.00

Winds of Change/Vientos de Cambio
bilingual poems Tomás Gayton
ISBN 0-9714003-6-9 $15.00

Change (will do you good)
by poet Gail Rudd Entrekin
ISBN 0-9714003-4-2 $15.00

Merge with the river
by Yosemite poet James Downs
ISBN 0-9714003-2-6 $14.00

Driven into the Shade
by Brandon Cesmat
2003 San Diego Book Award Poetry
ISBN 0-9714003-3-4 $14.00

dark hills and wild mountains
poems by john
ISBN 0-9714003-0-X $14.00

Solstice
by Kathryn Kruger
ISBN 0-9714003-1-8 $7.00

CPSIA information can be obtained at www.ICGtesting.com
Printed in the USA
LVOW01s1043010915

452364LV00036B/952/P